F♥RGIVENESS
IS NOT AN
OPTION

F♥RGIVENESS
IS NOT AN
OPTION

a journey to freedom and healing

ANNA MCCARTHY

AMBASSADOR INTERNATIONAL
GREENVILLE, SOUTH CAROLINA & BELFAST, NORTHERN IRELAND

www.ambassador-international.com

Forgiveness Is Not an Option
A Journey to Freedom and Healing

Printed in the United States of America

Print Edition: 978-1-62020-015-5
Electronic Edition: 978-1-62020-053-7

Cover Design and Page Layout by Matthew Mulder

AMBASSADOR INTERNATIONAL
Emerald House
427 Wade Hampton Blvd.
Greenville, SC 29609, USA
www.ambassador-international.com

AMBASSADOR BOOKS
The Mount
2 Woodstock Link
Belfast, BT6 8DD, Northern Ireland, UK
www.ambassador-international.com

The colophon is a trademark of Ambassador

This book is dedicated to:
Anne, Jannah, Melody, and Sarah
Thank you for allowing me to be me and for staying with me on the journey to finding who that was.

CONTENTS

PREFACE

Dear Reader,

This book was written over the course of some of the most painful yet joyful and freeing years of my life. Each chapter comes from a place of raw transparency through my personal journey to forgiveness and healing. Throughout this process, I asked many difficult questions and, in turn, learned much about myself and my Savior. I don't pretend to be a scholar or a well-trained psychologist; I am simply a person who was once held captive but is now set free.

There are two types of people who will read this book. The first is someone who is in the midst of great heartbreak and sorrow. You may be experiencing anger, loss, and hurt and read this in an attempt to find some solace and hope as you muddle through the tragedy in which you find yourself. The second is one who may not be walking in the immediate grip of tragedy. You may bear scars from your past, whether in childhood or adulthood, that seem to prevent you from moving forward. You may have noticed a pattern of broken relationships in your life that always result in the same ending. In whichever category you find yourself, at some point in your life you most likely have encountered someone you need to forgive. As you read through these pages, I encourage you to try not to focus on just one incident in your life but to be open to the broad spectrum of your life's events.

I subtitled this book "A journey to freedom and healing" because that is what I desire this to be for you—a journey. I would suggest you take one chapter at a time and try not to power through the entire book in one sitting! I encourage you to read this at your own pace and to journal while reading. At the close of each chapter, I have provided specific questions that I believe are paramount to the process. Journaling your thoughts will not only enable you to have a "space" to freely process what you are discovering but will also serve as a means to measure to your progress. There is nothing more encouraging than being able to look back over the course of even just a few weeks and see how far you've come! In the back of the book, you will find a reference list of Scriptures used in each chapter. This serves as a quick go-to in locating a verse without having to search the entire book.

My prayer for you is that you will embrace the truth of God's Word and allow it to be a guide as you begin to peel back the painful layers in your life, allowing the gift of forgiveness to heal your hurts. I cannot express to you the amount of joy and freedom you will discover once you open up and begin to embrace what God can do in you and through your situation, no matter how dark it may seem.

There is hope for you to be restored to wholeness again. I am a living, breathing testimony to this truth. Throughout the pages of this book are the key principles to unlocking that freedom, and at their core is the saving grace of Jesus Christ. Whether or not you consider yourself to be a follower of Jesus, or if you once were but are now in doubt, I can assure you—I understand where you are. Life has taught me over and over again just how unstable most things in this existence are. And, inevitably, we tend to put God in this category as well. But, there are two things I know for a fact—the wounds of your heart and life are real and won't disappear on their own, and God is the most stable Being in existence.

No matter where you stand in your beliefs, I ask you to consider what is written in the pages of this book with an open heart and mind. Whatever circumstance or situation led you to this point, I want you to know that freedom from the anger, loss, loneliness, and heartache is possible. Becoming a person free from fear and insecurity isn't simply possible, it's attainable. Join me on this journey, not only to experience healing from your wounds but also to begin living a life of freedom from them.

~ Anna

FORGIVENESS

Chapter 1

THE FUNERAL

When we experience the death of a loved one, we go through a process of grief. Anger, sadness, and loss typically run cycles through the course of an indeterminate amount of time until we finally arrive at acceptance. Death typically transpires with no one at fault. Other losses, however, are not as simple. They can include a loss of trust or innocence that comes with a person to blame. Betrayal and abuse can cause some of our greatest senses of personal loss. Other injuries, such as a broken relationship, marriage, or friendship, can leave painful scars that cripple nearly every area of our lives. You may not have experienced a loss due to a physical death, but somewhere in the midst of the injury, a part of you or your life was lost and on some level died.

There are many situations that can cause us to grieve, but we rarely give them the recognition they deserve. Personally, my greatest levels of grief have been experienced during seasons of broken relationships. Some were due to betrayal, broken trust, and abuse. Other relationships seemed to end without any reason at all and simply dissipated over time. However, one thing I have found woven through all of these situations is the need for validation. We all have an insatiable need to be heard and listened to, especially when we are hurting and grieving.

During one of these seasons, someone asked, "How are you handling your grief?" I about fell over because for a moment I thought that I had missed someone's death! But, after pausing, I understood; they were referring to my broken relationship. At first, I was offended that they had referred to it as though someone had died, yet as I pondered the words, I couldn't come up with anything else that more adequately described it. That relationship had in fact died, and whether I wanted to admit it or not, I was grieving the loss.

In my early twenties, I found myself as a single mother working two jobs just to make ends meet. Up until that point, I had rarely admitted my shortcomings or faults; I liked to appear as though I had everything together. Even when faced with tragedy, I somehow managed to "wow" everyone with my ability to cope and master the circumstance. I felt proud of this trait; it had been quite helpful on many occasions. Yet, during these years, it became increasingly difficult to push through as I had in the past. I cannot tell you the amount of irritation and frustration I felt as I tried repeatedly to overcome everything I had lost. After more failed attempts than I could count, I finally threw up my hands and admitted this was one battle I could not win.

This was the first moment in my life where no matter how much self-talking and self-medicating I administered, I could not for the life of me find joy in any part of my existence. Everything seemed hard, everything seemed foreign, and absolutely nothing was going my way. No matter how much I tried to do right, I still kept coming up with a long list of wrongs. I kept asking myself,

"Why am I not happy? Why do I *still* want to cry? Why out of no-where do I get angry?" I was able to ignore these questions for about two years—two very busy years. I forced myself to keep moving in order to keep my tower of strength facade from collapsing. Yet, in the quiet times, whether driving alone in my car or during my early morning shower, the house of cards would begin to fall, and out of nowhere floods of emotion and heartache came pouring out.

Of course, the tower of strength I ever-so-brilliantly built around myself would immediately quake and whisper words of condemnation, such as "What is wrong with you? Pull yourself together. You are fine; quit crying and get your act together." At times I would even echo this out loud to myself in a mad attempt to snap myself out of it. On occasion it would actually work—for a while. I would busy myself with work and activities, forcing myself to forget. But, before long, the rumbling would start up again. The pressure from locked up emotions would look for a crack in my walls through which to escape.

Then one day—an otherwise completely normal day—I arrived to the job I had been fervently working, made my coffee, sat down at my desk, and began to work just as I always had. I said hello to my co-workers, checked my make-up, and began my morning routine. The day had an odd feeling to it, though, and as I looked around, I noticed what was so strange. The office was quiet, unusually quiet. As I glanced down the hallway towards my boss's office, I noticed the other employees' doors were closed. Typically, every-one kept their office doors open unless they were in a meeting, and as I checked the schedule, I noted there were no meetings planned for that day. One by one the doors opened only for a mere moment as each employee went from office to office, continually closing the doors behind them. Hushed voices were followed by odd looks and swift movements as they hurried past my desk. Then, it happened. Silence was broken as I heard my name being called. As I walked toward my supervisor's office, I felt as though my heart were going to pound through my chest. What could possibly be happening? As I slowly walked down the hallway towards his office, I began preparing myself for the only thing I could think of; I was about to lose my job.

As I sat down at the conference table, I began to recall my past twelve months of work there. I had repeatedly received praises for my performance and had even been given a raise a few months earlier. What on earth could I have done to have disappointed the company so suddenly? As the words began flowing, my heart began to sink. There was no reason and no explanation; simply stated, my employment had been terminated. I questioned and advocated for an answer, yet none was given. They were simply "moving on." I managed to gain my composure long enough to gather my belongings and leave. As I stepped into the elevator and began the six-story descent, my little tower of strength began rapidly collapsing. How will I make rent this month? How will I pay for my daughter's school? How will I make my car payment? Dear God, why!?

As the elevator doors opened and I stepped into the parking garage, I could no longer hold the flood back. I began running to my car in order to maintain my composure until I was safely locked inside. As I climbed into my front seat, I fell apart. The tears were not only over the loss of my job and the fear of how we were going to survive, but over the loss of my life, my security, and my future as I thought it would be. I cried as though I were at a funeral, and for that moment, I was. I was at my funeral, feeling as if all hope had died.

The sadness turned into anger, which led to a whole gamut of emotions I had been attempting to ignore. I not only cried for the loss of my life as I had known it but also for the loss of myself. I hated who I had become. I was a stressed-out single parent who always worried about making ends meet, merely trying to survive each day. The joy I once had was a distant memory. All that remained was an empty shell of a person who had thrown herself into her job in order to escape from the reality of what her life had become. I didn't even know the person I had become, let alone like her. I grieved the loss of the innocent, free-spirited girl I had been, someone who had grown up to become a wonderful wife and mother who cherished every moment with her friends and family.

All of it seemed like a distant dream from which I had abruptly been awakened from, only to be plunged into a nightmare—a living nightmare that seemed endless. The colorful life I had once lived had faded to a dreary shade of grey where there was no joy or laughter. I cried for what seemed like hours. And each time I tried to regain composure, the sobs forced their way to the surface again. This was my funeral. Whether I wanted to admit it or not, the girl I had once been was not here anymore. The life I had once lived was gone. I was waking up to the reality of my life, and I did not like it. It wasn't fair, and it wasn't right. How could a just God have allowed this to happen? And, there it was; not only had I avoided acknowledging the brokenness of my life, I had also avoided acknowledging my broken relationship with God. After all, He had allowed this to happen! I thought, *Does he completely have it out for me, or what? He must have turned his back on me; He must not love me anymore.* I was alone. Truly alone. I hated who I had become and what my life had become. I felt like I was trapped in a prison with no way out. This was now who I was, and this was now my fate. This was the one battle that I could not win.

I don't know if reading this makes you uncomfortable or rings a bell of truth. But let me tell you, if you don't allow yourself to open up and be real about your situation and honest about your feelings toward it, you are going to end up just as I did: with years of un-resolved hurt and anger bombarding you when you least expect it, paralyzing you from being able to see past your situation. Not only that, but you will have one severely distorted view of your Heavenly Father, just as I did. Whether or not you are living this right now or are stuck in survival mode ignoring it, your emotions—left unat-tended from your loss—remain as they are. They will not fade or vanish simply because you tell them to. Believe me, I have tried! If you have suffered a loss, in order to truly move on, you must give it its proper validation. You must allow yourself to grieve.

So, how does one grieve? Truly, it seems like a simple enough project, but where does one begin? Very simply, you begin with a funeral. We have funerals when loved ones pass away. It's a time to reflect on their lives, their accomplishments, their traits that we grew to adore, and to give our final good-byes. You may have even attended a burial service where you watched as they lowered the coffin into the ground and covered it with dirt. Funerals are not joyous by any means, but they carry a weight of importance that helps us begin the grieving process. It gives us closure and allows us the opportunity to cry and mourn the loss of a life held so dear.

Other than a funeral, we typically do not give ourselves permission to be sad or to dwell on what has been lost. In our fast-paced lives, we push ourselves to keep moving and not look back. There is a time and place for that, but before you can pick up and move on, you must reflect and give your final goodbye.

In Deuteronomy 34:8 after Moses' death, it says, *"The Israelites grieved for Moses in the plains of Moab thirty days, until the time of weeping and mourning was over."* It struck me that they had a set time-frame for their grief. They allowed themselves a period of thirty days to grieve the loss of their leader. I don't know about you, but to me thirty days seems like a long time! Yet, in the entire span of our lives, why can't we allow ourselves at least thirty days to grieve our loss?

A passage I have come to appreciate is in John 16. Jesus began teaching his disciples about the grief they would experience upon his death. Now, his disciples had spent nearly every waking moment with Jesus during his ministry. They had walked with him, prayed with him, and devoted their entire lives to serving him. As you reflect upon the relationships in your life and their intimacy, imagine how much deeper the intimacy would be if it were with Jesus Christ himself. Our loss pales in comparison, yet I believe we can relate on some level to what the disciples were going to experience upon his death. Their source of strength and companionship was about to be brutally executed right in front of their eyes. How could one be prepared for that? How could one begin to cope with that loss? Jesus had insight on this as he began to foresee the heartache and pain they would endure. John 16:20-22 states, *"I tell you the truth, you will weep and mourn while the world rejoices. You will grieve, but your grief will turn to joy. A woman giving birth to a child has pain because her time has come; but when her baby is born she forgets the anguish because of her joy that a child is born into the world. So with you: Now is your time of grief, but I will see you again and you will rejoice, and no one will take away your joy."*

How incredible these words are! Read this verse again to yourself as though Jesus were speaking it directly to you. He tells you that you *will* weep and mourn, and that it is *okay*. My friend, Jesus himself has given you permission to grieve. Allow yourself to cry; allow yourself to mourn your loss.

He continues by telling you that your grief will turn to joy. This is *your* promise and *your* truth! Hold onto it with every ounce of fight that you have left in you. Just as in child birth, even though it is painful and many vow in the delivery room they will never do it again, they forget the pain once they take hold of that precious baby. Your joy may not come through a baby, but it will come through a gift. A gift that far surpasses any sort of life you thought you once had. God is standing by, waiting to pour out showers of blessings onto your life. But, you must let go and allow yourself to feel the pain before you can reap the reward. As he says in the latter portion of the verse, "Now is your time of grief, but I will see you again and you *will* rejoice, and no one will take away your joy." You will rejoice! Remember that innocent child you once were? You will become like that child again, and you will be seen by Jesus, and no one will be able to take away your joy on that day. This gift is for you.

The Lord will turn your grief into joy, but you must relinquish control, allowing him to be God and yourself to be human. Give your heart permission to be broken and to grieve. Once you open up and begin to be honest about your present state, you will face some difficult questions regarding your perspective of God, who he is to you, and what he has been doing in the midst of your pain and heartache. It's okay to wonder. Throughout the course of this book, we will discover some of the reasons why these things happen and how God can truly turn your broken life into one filled with peace and joy. And discover how, with his help, we can safeguard ourselves from a life lived in a perpetual cycle of loss.

I am committed to this journey with you. The pages of this book are a living, breathing testimony that what I am sharing with you is true. Begin this journey by giving your loss validation. Look at your loss and acknowledge the pain it has caused you. As hard as it may be, say your final goodbyes and lay it down. Allow yourself to grieve. We cannot receive from God when our hands are full of our burdens. Put your loss in the ground and open yourself up to the healing he wants to bring you.

"You *will* grieve, but your grief *will* turn to joy…"

Your Journey. . .

1.   In what areas of your life have you experienced a loss or heartache?

2.   How have you allowed yourself to grieve?

3.   Who has God been to you in the midst of these circumstances?

4.   List these areas and the pain their absence has inflicted on you.

5. Ask God to show you if you need to give any of these a "funeral" and if so, what it should look like. Express your thoughts here.

6. Pray that the Lord will help you to say your final "good-byes" and begin to write them here.

F♥RGIVENESS

Chapter 2

REJECTION OR REDEMPTION?

In the previous chapter, I proposed that our release begins with a funeral. I shared with you what my personal "funeral" was; what yours will look like will be unique to you and to your situation. For some, it is simply allowing yourself time to reflect on what was lost—giving yourself permission to remember the good and the bad of what you are leaving behind and what that void feels like. You may prefer to do this alone or with a close friend. You may choose to reflect out loud, on paper, or quietly to yourself. Tears may come, whether from joy as you reflect on the good that was lost or from anger or heartache at the injustice you faced. Once given its proper recognition, I encourage you to have a personal ceremony. This may include throwing away items that are left from the past, putting pictures away that no longer need to be a constant reminder of your loss, or burning a letter or item and burying its ashes to symbolize the closure and finality of its exit from your life.

As you process the loss that you are grieving, I encourage you to try and retrace its path back to where the initial injury or hurt occurred. Once you arrive, you may find that rejection is present. Rejection tries to make us believe that we fell short because we were not worthy of being accepted, loved, or respected. If we believe this lie, we become convinced that we can never measure up to the standards set before us. We will suspect that once those whom we love get close to us, they will discover what everyone else already has—that we aren't good enough.

All of us lend ourselves to a specific coping mechanism when experiencing feelings of rejection. Whether we are aware of it or not, we all tend to hide in a familiar activity or practice in order to keep from facing the reality of our situation. We gravitate toward what we can control in order to escape from what we cannot. When experiencing rejection, I run to cleaning. I organize closets, scrub bathroom floors, wash mattress pads, quilts—you name it, I clean it. When that is done, I usually move on to household projects such as painting cabinet doors, hanging new light fixtures, changing out hardware, moving furniture, or redecorating a room. This is how I cope. I lose myself in "projects" that I know how to do well. If I surround myself with one accomplishment after another, I'm distracted from the part life where I feel like I've failed. In every voice of rejection, failure is a ready accomplice, attempting to convince us that we have failed somehow in our efforts to keep what we had or what we thought we had. Once the failure card has been played, all sense of security and self-worth go flying out the window. In sweeps rejection, wrapping itself around you like a heavy blanket and pulling you even deeper into despair.

It isn't long before your feelings of rejection from not being good enough bleed into every other aspect of your life. Before you know it, you begin analyzing every relationship, trying to piece to-gether those who haven't rejected you from those who have or those who one day could. You become a shrewd detective, and in your mind you begin to piece together the unsolved mysteries of every-one who has hurt you, and you are determined to protect yourself from ever letting it happen again. You question those who "seem" to be innocent but are surely going to be found guilty soon.

This over-protective game is nothing more than a way for you to sink deeper into the prison that rejection has already built and to barricade yourself in. You begin saying to yourself, *Surely if the walls are thick enough, no one can see how vulnerable I am; if the locks are strong enough, no one can break in and find me. Savior? What Savior?! I am in a panicked, every-man-for-himself mode!*

Those who may try to approach you would find themselves quickly rejected as well. In taking a readily defensive posture, you may respond, saying things like "Don't you dare question me. You don't know me, you don't know my story; you haven't been where I've been; you haven't suffered like I have. God obviously forgot about me a long time ago. Look at what he let happen! I am now completely alone thanks to his plan. Yes, I am angry at God—I am furious! Look at everyone else who has happy, fulfilling lives, and they don't even know God! I go to church, I read my Bible, I did everything just as he wanted me to, and look what he did to me! You don't know what I've been through. So, back off and leave me alone!"

The above passage comes from a journal entry of mine from years ago. It pains me that I wrote these words, but what is more painful is how deeply I felt them. Thoughts like this are what begin to take up residence in the crevices of our minds and taunt us at will. This is usually what we are attempting to run away from. I don't know what stage you find yourself in right now, but I can tell you I've been there through every stage, and just when I thought I was done, the drums would roll, the curtains would open, and the scene would start all over again. No matter what your current situation is, one fact remains the same for everyone. You are exhausted; exhausted from hiding, fearing, crying, doubting, fighting, trying desperately to pull everything back together again, yet undoubtedly finding yourself running in circles back to where you started. Let me assure you that you are not alone. I was the queen of this cycle. However, after running for a few years, I finally waved the white flag and quit running.

If we are not careful, the painful journeys we go through can ruin the glorious good that our Savior wants to bring out of them. And, yes, I said "good." Believe me, there is actual good that can come from the hole you are attempting to climb out of. While I don't know your situation or your pain or how you have suffered, God does. The mighty Creator of this entire universe actually knows what you are going through and wants to bring good out of it and bless you with a life even more fulfilling than the one you are wishing you had. How can he do this? This, my friend, is called redemption.

We've all heard about it, know about it, and talk about it as though it were second nature to us. Whether in church, in song lyrics, or in Scripture, this concept of redemption has become something we take lightly. It occurred to me that this word must have a powerful affect not only on my salvation but also on my daily walk with Christ. Most of us already know on the surface what redemption means; yet, many of us more readily identify with being one who is rejected rather than redeemed. Why is that?

Let's start by looking at what these two words actually mean. The word "rejection" means *to throw out as useless or worthless; to refuse to accept, acknowledge, use, or believe. Something rejected as imperfect, unsatisfactory, or useless.* Sound familiar? This has failure written all over it! Yet, what is amazing is that in Christ we are defined as the exact opposite of this word. Scripture tells us that we have been redeemed. In contrast, the word "redeem" means: *to recover possession or ownership of by payment of a price or service; to reinstate someone's estimation or good opinion; to restore to favor: to make amends for or to recover from captivity.*

As you read those two definitions, which would you say adequately describes you in your present state or in some previous situation? Which one identifies more with your feelings and emotions currently? When faced with a betrayal, loss, or grievance, do you run to redemption, or do you hide in rejection?

Nearly all of us will face rejection in one way or another, especially on the tail end of a betrayal or heartbreak. The problem I find is that many of us continue to stay rooted to that point in time, never completely moving past it. We lose touch with who we are in Christ and begin identifying more with what our past experiences tell us we are, falling for the lies of the enemy. We accept the lie that tells us we are not good enough, we are failures, and we are completely unworthy of love and acceptance. The truth is that in Christ we are not failures and are deeply and profoundly loved.

Romans 8:37-39 tells us, *"No, in all these things we are more than conquerors through him who **loved us**. For I am convinced that neither death nor life, neither angels nor demons, neither the present nor the future, nor any powers, neither height nor depth, nor anything else in all creation, will be able to separate us from the love of God that is in Christ Jesus our Lord."*

Jeremiah 31:31 speaks to the gravity of this love, saying, *"I have **loved** you with an **everlasting love**; I have drawn you with unfailing kindness"* (emphasis mine).

Instead of addressing the lies from the enemy in contrast with the truth of God's Word, we accept the lie. We throw ourselves into coping mode, merely trying to survive, and swim through the emotional turmoil we are experiencing, trying to keep our head above water.

None of us wish to go through the pain of rejection. We do everything in our power to protect ourselves. We are swift to make mental notes on how to avoid that pain again and prepare our "game plan" in order to secure our safety. In theory, this sounds plausible. Yet, without redemption, this method offers only a false sense of security. True, the surface emotions may fade, but if not fully "redeemed" in Christ, they will inevitably return to the surface when provoked or threatened—mostly due to our natural instinct of self-defense and self-preservation. You may find that you continue to rotate through the rejection cycle, often landing back in the same scenario that led you to rejection in the first place, cycling you back to where you started or leaving you completely alone in an attempt to avoid any sense of vulnerability.

Most of us would agree that, given the choice between rejection and redemption, we would choose redemption. So, after salvation, what does living a redeemed life look like? Well, take the situation(s) that you are currently facing. Imagine that situation being recovered and restored to wholeness. Not externally, but internally. What would it look like if every space in your heart that had felt broken and empty was restored, made whole, and filled again? What if every square inch of your mind, emotion, and soul that had been held captive to that situation were to be completely set free?

Being redeemed is having someone pay a price for your pain and imprisonment, giving you freedom in return. Would you believe me if I said this is what Jesus did for us on the cross? Many of us believe he died for our sins so that we wouldn't be held captive by sin any longer. This is true enough, as this is what occurs during salvation. But we forget that it doesn't stop there. In this world, we are not only bound by our own sin but also by the sins of others who have left us crippled by rejection or abuse. Our Savior and Redeemer died (paying the price) to redeem us from the captivity that our minds and emotions endure due to the pain others have inflicted on us. Isaiah 61:1-3 prophesies of what Jesus was coming to the earth to do:

> *The Spirit of the Sovereign LORD is on me,*
> *because the LORD has anointed me*
> *to proclaim good news to the poor.*
> *He has sent me to bind up the brokenhearted,*
> *to proclaim freedom for the captives*
> *and release from darkness for the prisoners,*

> *to proclaim the year of the LORD's favor*
>   *and the day of vengeance of our God,*
> *to comfort all who mourn,*
>   *and provide for those who grieve in Zion—*
> *to bestow on them a crown of beauty*
>   *instead of ashes,*
> *the oil of joy*
>   *instead of mourning,*
> *and a garment of praise*
>   *instead of a spirit of despair.*

Notice the picture he paints with these words: the broken-hearted, captives, prisoners, all who mourn, those who grieve. This describes the difficult seasons of life. God says that he will give us beauty instead of ashes (restoration), joy instead of mourning (wholeness/repair), and praise instead of despair. This is the heart of our Savior. When Jesus died, his death paid the price necessary to draw us into freedom—if we are willing to accept it.

One of my favorite people in the Bible is Job. His story may tend to be overlooked as the book by his name is filled with many chapters that describe all of the heartache, pain, grief, and loss that this world has to offer. Many of us tend to shy away from these topics; we are usually more apt to focus on cleaning rather than reading Job when we are suffering! However, there is much to be learned from Job, specifically in this area.

In Job chapter 19, Job tells of his unrelenting pain and loss. He shares about being alienated from his family and relatives, being forgotten by his friends, being stripped of all honor and justice, and how even the breath out of his mouth was offensive to his wife. He describes little children hurling ridicule at him. Everyone he loved had turned against him. In verse 20, he says, *"I am nothing but skin and bones."* I can't help but think that these words were not meant figuratively; his flesh and bones were literally all that was left of his life on earth. His "friends" at the time were voicing continual judgment towards Job throughout the pages of the book. They were determined that he had been in error (or failed) in some area of his life, which was why he was being punished by God.

Ring a bell? The enemy used the failure card even back in Job's day! This game has been played over and over again, but I dare say that the hand dealt to Job took rejection and failure to a completely new low. Even in his suffering, no comfort was to be found. He had no one; he was utterly alone in his misery, combating heavy loads of criticism. If anyone had ever met rejection face to face, it was Job. Yet, we see the heart of Job expressed as a man who in the face of adversity did not lose sight of who God was. In verses 23-27, Job pours out the cry of his heart:

Oh, that my words were recorded,
that they were written on a scroll,
that they were inscribed with an iron tool on lead,
or engraved in rock forever!
I know that my redeemer lives,
and that in the end he will stand on the earth.
And after my skin has been destroyed,
yet in my flesh I will see God;
I myself will see him

with my own eyes—I, and not another.
How my heart yearns within me!"

I love how Job wanted these words to be the ones that were "engraved in rock forever." He wanted it to be known where he stood on the matter of his life, his loss, his rejection, and his grief. He proclaimed, "I know that my redeemer lives and in the end he will stand on the earth." Notice the words he didn't say. He didn't say, "My God lives" or "My Savior lives." He chose to say, "My Redeemer lives." He took ownership of his right standing with God and his place as God's child. He didn't buy into the lie that he was a failure or that he had been forgotten by God. Instead, he confidently stood on the promise we read in Isaiah. Job even took it one step further by saying that even if the only thing he had left (his skin and bones) was destroyed, he knew that redemption would come. Even if it came in death, he knew he would see God with his own eyes. He knew who God was and who God wasn't. God was his Redeemer, plain and simple. He was a chosen and loved child of God. Nearly every facet of his life was screaming the opposite at him, yet his confidence in who he was in God remained steadfast. Job managed to keep a proper perspective despite the tragedy he faced.

How sobering this is! My heart longs to be rooted that deeply in the promise we have in our Redeemer. And for most of us, it isn't a matter of hearing it; it is a matter of believing it. We have bought into the enemy's lie so many times that the truth can sound unbelievable—incredible, even. Like Job, when all those voices throw lies at us, we must cling to the truth and proclaim our status as sons and daughters of God. We are not rejected people—rendered useless failures who must spend our lives in hiding. No, as sons and daughters of God, we are redeemed! Jesus paid the price for us to live redeemed lives, not rejected lives. We have value in his sight! Praise the Lord!

In your pain, I encourage you to thank him for what he did for you. Take comfort from Job chapter 19. By earthly standards, Job wasn't anyone special; he was human just like every one of us. The only difference is that he chose to stand with confidence on the promises of God, while most of us let doubts steal away our confidence. You don't have to "feel" free just yet to begin declaring your freedom. I doubt Job "felt" redeemed during those days of physical and emotional suffering. When you begin to feel the lies of rejection creeping in, stand on the truth. You are more than a conqueror in Christ, and you ARE loved with an everlasting love! I encourage you to write Isaiah 61:1-3 down and put it in a place where you will continually see it. Meditate on it and try to begin viewing yourself not as a rejected person but as a redeemed child of God. Follow Job's lead and proclaim with your mouth, "I know my Redeemer lives!"

If you find yourself not knowing what to pray, I encourage you to try praying Scripture. This can be such a powerful tool! As we close this chapter, I encourage you to pray the following verses, found in Lamentations 3:54-58.

The waters closed over my head,
   and I thought I was about to perish.
I called on your name, LORD,
   from the depths of the pit.

You heard my plea: "Do not close your ears
   to my cry for relief."

You came near when I called you,
   and you said, "Do not fear."
You, Lord, took up my case;
   you redeemed my life.

Your Journey. . .

1. As you process the loss that you are grieving, try and retrace its path back to where the initial injury occurred. What "rejection" lie were you told?

2. How do you typically cope with rejection?

3. As you read the two definitions of rejection and redemption, which would you say adequately describes you in your present state or even in a previous situation? Which one identifies more with your feelings and emotions currently? When faced with a betrayal, loss, or grievance, do you run to redemption or hide in rejection?

4. Imagine your heart in these areas being restored to wholeness. What would that look like? What in your life would change?

5. What comfort do you take from Job chapter 13?

6. Write Isaiah 61:1-3 down and put it in a place where you will continually see it. Meditate on it and try to begin viewing yourself not as a rejected person but as a redeemed child of God.

Chapter 3

TO THE ABUSED

This particular chapter is reserved for those who have been wounded by serious acts of abuse or neglect. If you have not experienced mistreatment of this nature, you can move on to the next chapter. However, if abuse has characterized any portion of your life, no matter how many years may have passed since it last occurred, I encourage you to read on.

It doesn't matter how long ago the abuse occurred. You can't escape the aftermath. It creates shock waves that continue to ripple throughout the course of one's life. Regardless of the difference in circumstances, victims of abuse tend to carry many of the same emotional scars throughout life. We feel unworthy, mistrusting, scared, and—ultimately—alone. For me personally, the isolation that comes with abuse was the most difficult to bear.

I was raised in a wonderfully God-fearing home with parents for whom I am so thankful. I grew up in church. On many levels I was a bit sheltered, which in many ways I have come to appreciate. Yet, when confronted with sexual abuse as a child, I found myself helpless, not knowing how to cope. Sexual abuse wasn't talked about in church; there weren't sermons titled "what to do when someone molests you." In those days, many parents weren't aware of the dangers that existed and weren't talking to their children about how to avoid or report sexual abuse. So, when it happened to me, I felt lost, wondering where God was in all of that mess and what on earth I was supposed to do with the damage that had been left because of it.

In my early adulthood, I found myself in an abusive relationship that included more sexual abuse, along with something that until this point I had been unfamiliar with: domestic violence. Feeling a punch in the stomach for the first time was a rude awakening to the callousness that exists within the broken people of this world. Being spat upon and laughed at as I lay crumpled in pain was something no sermon could have prepared me for. Being humiliated to the point of degradation almost killed me—literally. At that moment, the message that I was not worthy of being treated with respect and, more significantly, that I couldn't count on anyone to take care of me, had been firmly cemented in my mind. I was alone. Very, very alone. I adopted a mentality that no one could take care of me but me. No one could protect me but me. I believed that God was either unaware of my situation or else didn't care.

When I became a mother, this insatiable fear took hold of me. Terror that my child would fall prey to the same types of people whose abuse had eroded my heart and mind into a crippling state. I could not bear the thought of her experiencing that pain and abuse. I was leery of meeting new people, didn't let her attend sleepovers, and kept her very close. There were nights I remember repeatedly checking on her in her room as she slept—just to reassure my mind that she was safe.

Your experiences may have led you to a similar frame of mind. Some of you have experienced even greater injuries. Whether major or minor, abuse leaves you undone and tormented until healing takes place. As someone who has walked this path, I encourage you to recognize that you are not alone and that healing is possible. If you have not sought counseling, I highly recommend that you do so. Many church organizations offer excellent resources in this area. If you're like me, you may shy away from wanting to talk about it or ask for help. When you take that step, you may be surprised to find how many people are out there are just like you.

Having that said, let me resume my story. After the abuse had ended, I remember sitting in church and feeling lost and confused. Although I was singing the songs I had sung my entire life, my heart was calloused and closed off to just about everything. What was left of me was not much more than a shell, but whatever was left inside my heart, it needed to know who God really was. What his opinion of abuse was—if he was aware of it, and if he was, what was he going to do about it.

I cracked open my Bible and looked up everything I could on the subject. Surprisingly, God has much to say on the matter. I learned much about who our God is, but I also learned much about myself as I began to see myself through his eyes, not only as someone who had been deeply wronged but also as someone whom he cares for deeply and longs to protect.

The book of Psalms resonated greatly with me. I have come to have great affection for David in Scripture; he has become so easy to relate to. He has a way of putting things into words that speaks to my heart. And, as a "man after God's own heart," David wrote in Psalm 119:78 of his own battle in the area of abuse:

> *May they be put to shame for wronging me without cause...*

When you are wronged for no reason, like David describes here, it is not only shocking but ultimately devastating. The endless wonderings of *"why?"* and *"what did I do to deserve this?"* permeate your mind at a staggering rate. I imagine this is what prompted David to pray this way.

There is another passage in Psalms that, when I first read it, seemed to jump off the page. Beginning in Psalm chapter 10, we read David's description of an abuser:

> *Why, LORD, do you stand far off?*
> *Why do you hide yourself in times of trouble?*
>
> *In his arrogance the wicked man hunts down the weak,*
> *who are caught in the schemes he devises.*
> *He boasts about the cravings of his heart;*
> *he blesses the greedy and reviles the LORD.*
> *In his pride the wicked man does not seek him;*
> *in all his thoughts there is no room for God.*
> *His ways are always prosperous;*
> *your laws are rejected by him;*
> *he sneers at all his enemies.*
> *He says to himself, "Nothing will ever shake me."*
> *He swears, "No one will ever do me harm."*
>
> *His mouth is full of lies and threats;*

trouble and evil are under his tongue.
He lies in wait near the villages;
  from ambush he murders the innocent.
His eyes watch in secret for his victims;
  like a lion in cover he lies in wait.
He lies in wait to catch the helpless;
  he catches the helpless and drags them off in his net.
 His victims are crushed, they collapse;
  they fall under his strength.
 He says to himself, "God will never notice;
  he covers his face and never sees."

(Psalm 10:1-11)

Verses 9-10 particularly grabbed my attention. This describes every abuser I have known and the gravity of what they do to those they injure. *"His victims are crushed, they collapse; they fall under his strength."* David did not mince words; he was not making a pretty picture out of this at all. This is the reality of the abused and the abuser. At one point or another, we are crushed and fall under the abuser's strength. And, the abuser seemingly does it to spite God. Under the heavy weight of this reality, David cries out to God on behalf of the victims.

Psalm 10:14-15 says:

"But you, God, see the trouble of the afflicted;
  you consider their grief and take it in hand.
The victims commit themselves to you;
  you are the helper of the fatherless.

Break the arm of the wicked man;
  call the evildoer to account for his wickedness
  that would not otherwise be found out."

He begins by acknowledging that God himself sees the *"trouble of the afflicted"* and *"consider(s) their grief."* This right here tells us that any misguided thoughts we have about God being unaware of our torment is false. He not only sees it, but he takes control of the situation. Right away David addresses the need for victims to commit themselves to God, and he immediately gives the reason behind it: "you (God) are the helper of the fatherless." Culturally, a father is someone who is supposed to protect his children. I like to read this as "you are the helper of those *without someone to protect them*." Not only is God aware of our abuse, but if we commit ourselves to him, he promises to help us.

I absolutely love verse 15. Again, David isn't leaving anything unaddressed in this matter! He directly asks God to "break the arm" of the abuser and call him to account for his behavior "that would not otherwise be found out." Secrecy and hiding always seem to accompany abuse. Why? So that the abuser is not found out, exposed, and brought to justice. Knowing this, David cries out for God to expose the abuser and the abuse.

In the last few verses, David reveals his trust in the Lord. God is not a God to be mocked. He is a God who fulfills his promises, and David boldly proclaimed them.

"The LORD is King for ever and ever;
    the nations will perish from his land. You, LORD, hear the
desire of the afflicted;
    you encourage them, and you listen to their cry,
defending the fatherless and the oppressed,
    so that mere earthly mortals
    will never again strike terror."

(Psalm 10:16-18)

Throughout this entire passage, you can almost hear the desperation in David's voice as he speaks these words. Deeply grieved by the wickedness of the people in his day, he petitioned aggressively for God's justice. He declared God's sovereignty as a powerful defender of the oppressed. He proclaimed that the Lord is the only King—no abuser stands a chance in the presence of God's authority. He reaffirmed that the Lord hears the desires of the afflicted, encourages them, and listens to their cry. Take courage from this. When you cry out to God, he hears you. He is still listening to you. He promises to *"defend the fatherless and the oppressed,"* or as I like to read it, *"defend those without protection and the abused"* so that *"mere earthly mortals will never again strike terror."*

You must remember that God is God. Anyone else is merely a human being, incapable of the power that comes from God alone. You have that very same powerful God ready and waiting to listen, encourage, comfort, defend, and heal you.

But I will restore you to health and heal
your wounds, declares the Lord,
because you are called an outcast, Zion for whom no one cares.

(Jeremiah 30:17)

When we commit our lives to the Lord, he promises to not only hear us and defend us but also heal us—his ultimate gift to the abused. This gift is readily available for you and begins when you surrender your entirety to Him and allow him to be King of your life—not fear, not your past, and certainly not your abuser.

I close this chapter with great humility, as I cannot know your pain. But, I do know God, and I have experienced his healing in the area of abuse. My heart longs for you to find that same rest. His heart breaks for your suffering and is filled with righteous fury at the injustice you have faced. His desire is never for us to be tormented or abused. If you are in an abusive situation currently, you do not have to stay there. Your safety is of utmost importance; safe houses and shelters are available for those in need of refuge. Call your local police station or hospital for help locating a safe house in your area.

As difficult as it may seem at times, I've found forgiveness is the key to healing. Is that asking too much of you? Your shattered heart may think so. Please know that I desire your healing and the ultimate freedom that can only be found in Jesus. I want to be sensitive to the nature of your brokenness, which is why I felt it necessary to address you personally. My desire isn't for you to be merely a survivor—it's for you to thrive, wholly restored. And, from what I've found, thriving isn't possible without the healing hands of Jesus.

Believe. Allow him to guide you. God is good; he will see you through this journey.

You will not find any questions at the end of this chapter, as I feel they are not needed. Take this chapter as a personal note from one victim of abuse to another. I pray it has encouraged your heart and offered reassurance that you are not walking this journey alone. There is hope for you and your situation, no matter how grievous or dark. God can and will restore you to wholeness again.

FORGIVENESS

Chapter 4

THE INSTEADS

The Lord not only desires to redeem us, but he longs to completely restore what was lost. Our key passage, Isaiah 61:1-3, describes him as giving us a "crown of beauty *instead* of ashes, the oil of gladness *instead* of mourning, and a garment of praise *instead* of a spirit of despair." How beautiful this picture is! In order for the Lord to begin restoring us, we must come to a place of complete surrender. And, complete surrender inevitably involves brokenness. Before the Lord can begin restoring what has been stolen or lost, we must become like David in Psalm 31:11-13.

Because of all my enemies,
I am the utter contempt of my neighbors
and an object of dread to my closest friends—
those who see me on the street flee from me.
I am forgotten as though I were dead;
I have become like broken pottery.

This verse served as the inspiration for this book and completely describes the point at which I found myself, that pushed me to surrender my entirety to the Lord. I took all of my pain and the mess of my situation and gave it to the only One who had the authority and ability to turn my heap of ashes into something beautiful. In this verse, David had come to that very same place. He described himself as "broken pottery." When you break pottery, it is nearly impossible to piece back together. And, even if you are able to repair it, the seams where it has been glued together will be apparent. There is no humanly possible way to restore broken pottery back to its original, whole state. The same is true with us. Apart from God, we, like broken pottery, are unable to be restored. David, in essence, was declaring his brokenness. He was telling the Lord that there was no way he could be made whole again. He was broken beyond repair. As he writes further on in Psalm 51:17, *"My sacrifice, O God, is a **broken spirit**; a **broken** and contrite heart you, God, will not despise."*

David did what most of us would tend to shy away from. He offered the Lord his broken spirit as a *sacrifice*! We are so caught up in trying to keep it all "together" in front of people that, out of habit, we fail to be fully transparent with God. But David, in spite of his suffering, managed to maintain a proper perspective. He kept people in their place and recognized God's place. He acknowledged that God already knew the depths of his heart; instead of hiding what was inside, he gave full disclosure! Not only that, but he also took it one step further by presenting his brokenness to the Lord as his sacrifice, standing on the promise that God would not despise his heart.

The glorious part about this exercise in faith is that once we sacrifice our brokenness to the Lord, we allow him to release full restoration into our lives! Although subtle at first, you will begin seeing the "insteads" starting to appear—some of which may have already been present.

The moment I began to fully realize this truth working in my own life was breathtaking. This is the portion of my story where I allowed the Lord into my brokenness; he opened my eyes to see my pain from his perspective and began to show me all of the "insteads" he had already begun giving me. Gently taking my hand, he guided me to continue to open up to him and trust him even more, thus opening the floodgates of healing, releasing my heart from its captivity. Had it not been for this moment, much of my life would not be as it is today. Externally, not much would seem different, yet internally a brewing storm would still reside—much different from the peace I am fully experiencing now. Subtle—yet vastly different.

I lived in Missouri most of my teen and young adult years. Unfortunately, those were some of the most gut-wrenching years of my life to date. I live in Kansas now. In many ways, living across the state line has been therapeutic for me. If and when I need to go to the Missouri "side" (as we call it), I carefully plan my route so that I can avoid certain areas of town that may trigger a memory for me that I would prefer not to remember. Places are very monumental to me and always have been. For instance, I spent my childhood in Nashville, TN. I can't go back to Nashville without visiting my childhood home. It floods my mind with every childhood memory I have—it's as though I am innocent and young all over again and have every wish and dream at my fingertips. I absolutely love going back there. Unfortunately, the same is true of some places in my early adulthood—and those are places that I do not wish to revisit.

When I visit there, the memories are so readily accessible and the emotions are just as raw as they were the last time I was there; it can cause mere breathing to be painful.

Then came the fateful day when I had to face my Missouri "demons." On that particular day, I was driving to a friend's home in Missouri. From my house in Kansas, I can take a certain route that takes me around the city to avoid the unpleasant places. However, my mom was keeping my girls for me that day, so I was coming from her part of town instead. From her house, the only way to get there was to travel the route that would take me exactly where I didn't want to go.

I gathered my courage, prayed, and trusted God to get me through without a major emotional meltdown. As I drove, I kept the radio on. In trying to keep my mind busy, I continued praying and talking to God while listening. Soon, I was in the area where I had lived throughout high school. I could see my parents' old neighborhood where I had lived and where I had met my ex-husband. Within an instant, all of the memories from that "place" came rushing back. The good ones that hurt, and the painful ones that hurt even more. One particular memory sprang forward. I had not spoken about it or thought of it in years. It was the moment when I realized my marriage was truly over.

On that particular night, all of my hopes for my marriage and family being restored had shattered, and the walls of my broken and bleeding heart began to cave in. In a rush of panic and a desperate need to escape the pain, lies, and betrayal, I grabbed my keys and headed out the door. I didn't know where I was going, and I didn't care. I just knew I had to leave. As I was driving out of that ever-so-familiar neighborhood, I had to pull over. My uncontrollable tears prevented me from seeing straight, and I could barely catch my breath between sobs. This was the moment I physically felt my heart break. I looked out my car window at the ditch on the side of my car and wanted with everything within me to crawl into that ditch and just lie there. It was the lowest position I could think of. Somehow, it completely represented the way I felt inside.

As this memory flooded my mind, my eyes immediately began welling up with tears ... how I had forgotten that moment. How it angered me to remember it! Where had God been THAT night?

As I continued on my route, another painful memory made its way to the surface. There was a period in my life where I was a victim of domestic violence. When the abuse would take place, I would typically retreat to a bathroom, lock the door, and lie on the cold floor crying, praying for help, praying for relief, and begging God for an answer. Those moments were very isolating and are the few moments that I can honestly say I felt one hundred percent alone: no one to call, no one to run to, no one to confide in—complete and utter loneliness. How many times had I sat in bathrooms praying and waiting for relief that never came? Remembering this pained and angered me in the same way the last memory had.

I found myself driving at least fifteen miles over the speed limit, just trying to get to my friend's house as fast as I possibly could. I now realized why I had avoided those places. I didn't want to confront my broken state. I was free of those situations, yet my heart and mind were still being held captive by them, bound in chains at the very thought of what had once been. In facing those memories, I could not deny my brokenness. At that moment, a song came on the radio titled "Something Beautiful." The lyrics were ironic, considering my emotional state at the time. And that's when God finally spoke. My sweet Heavenly Father gently began speaking to me. He had wanted me to revisit all of those memories so that he could set me free from the prison in which they had kept me. Psalm 34:18 says, *"The LORD is close to the brokenhearted and saves those who are crushed in spirit."*

He drew close to me during that moment as he began opening my mind, revealing his heart to me. Mine had been broken for years, and so had his. He began to make known how deep his love and desire was to rescue me. Immediately, my mind flashed back to the ditch on the side of that road. And as the song played, my mind's eye saw my Savior scoop me up out of that ditch and run away with me. My mind then darted to the bathroom floor and to my tear-stained face as Christ himself broke down the door and came to my rescue. Picking up my broken body, he carried me softly to safety.

As I soaked all of this in, my heart began to swell with joy. He HAD been there and WAS with me. And, had he been physically present on Earth, I believe He loves me enough that He physically would have done those things for me. I began to see what Christ saw in those moments. I began to feel his jealous love for me. I felt justice in His arms and the strength to make all things right. I saw His passionate desire to rescue me. For the first time, I was able to look back on those moments and not feel shame. I felt desired— passionately desired. I felt worthy of being rescued.

However, as a woman—and as the eternal dreamer I seem to be—I couldn't help but ask all of the whys. If I was so special to God, why wasn't I enough for my husband? If the God of the entire universe cherished me to that extent, why didn't my abusers cherish me? Why had those years ended so tragically? One of the things I have truly appreciated over the years is how honest we can be with God. I love that I can confidently approach the throne of God and ask these questions without condemnation or fear of being reprimanded. While sitting in my car, the Lord quietly spoke these words to me: "Yes, some of your dreams did die. But, look at what you have *instead*." My hands, still a bit shaky, touched my five-month's-pregnant belly. I wept with joy as I looked at everything God had given me "instead." Yes, my first marriage had ended, but now I am in a marriage built on the foundation of the Lord. For years, I was unable to conceive a baby physically—a very painful process to walk through. But, we adopted our precious daughter whom I know for certain the Lord had planned for our family. That child has ministered to me more than I have pages for in this book! During that season of my life, God gave me her instead of a pregnancy and, oh, how thankful I am that He did! Then, God gave me the joy of a second healthy pregnancy with my husband Zac, and what a precious gift carrying these babies has been. Many times we can get so wrapped up in everything that has been lost or taken from us that we completely miss all of the blessings that the Lord has given us instead.

The Lord desperately longs to bring us beauty *instead* of ashes, gladness *instead* of mourning, and praise *instead* of despair. And, he does this by scooping up our broken pieces and doing what only he can do—restoring them into something more beautiful than they were before. Whatever false ideas you have about being able to be broken before the Lord, I encourage you to lay your pride aside and follow David's lead. Allow yourself to be broken, allow yourself to fall apart, and instead of wallowing in it or running and hiding from it, offer it to the Lord as a sacrifice. His Word promises you that he will not despise you! He will actually draw *closer* to you because of it!

Now, some of you may be thinking, "Well, that's great that you've been given some things in place of what you had lost, but that's not the case for me. I am sitting in a pile of nothingness. There isn't anything good in my situation right now, nor can I see any good coming from it in the future. It's completely void and empty." I walked through hell and back through those years, and the Lord has graciously bestowed restoration to my life in many areas. Yet, I can humbly stand before you today and say that Christ has given me all of the "insteads" out of his mercy for me *because* of my willingness to be broken before him. God can't fix someone who refuses to admit he or she is broken.

My encouragement to you, in whatever stage you find yourself on this journey, is that you sit and simply ask the Lord to remind you of places in your life that are broken. (Some of us readily know what they are, and others know that they are there but need a reminder about how to pinpoint them.) Something is broken when it simply isn't working right. What are the broken areas in your life? Explore them with the Lord and ask him to give you the grace to be humble and transparent before him. Admit your weakness; admit your inability to fix them on your own. Cry out to God as David did and openly declare your broken state. Then, ask the Lord to begin shifting your focus to view these areas from his perspective. Ask him to open your mind to see your life through his eyes. Ask him to reveal his passionate love and desire for your wholeness in these areas. God's Word promises us that if we seek him with all of our heart, we will find him. You can rest assured by that promise that he will draw near to you and will be found by you.

I am a testimony to this truth. How beautiful is the love the Lord has for us! I am in awe of his goodness. He has taken what was barren and desolate and made vineyards, valleys, and rivers flow. He will restore to you what once was lost. Meditate on Isaiah 61 and let the true heart of your Redeemer sink in.

Your Journey. . .

1. What are the broken areas in your life? (*Remember, a broken area is simply something that isn't working right.*) Write them down and ask the Lord to give you the grace to be humble and transparent.

2. How have you tried to fix these areas in your own strength? Have you surrendered these areas to God, declaring your brokenness and inability to repair them on your own?

3. Journal your cry to God as David did, openly declaring your broken state, modeling Psalm 51:17 (*"My sacrifice, O God, is a **broken spirit**; a **broken** and contrite heart you, God, will not despise"*).

4. *Ask the Lord to begin shifting your focus to view these areas from his perspective. Ask him to open your mind to see your*

life through his eyes. Ask him to reveal his passionate love and desire for your wholeness in these areas. Write your thoughts.

5. What are some of the "insteads" in your life?

6. As you meditate on Isaiah 61, what impact does this passage have on you?

FORGIVENESS

Chapter 5

BROKEN PEOPLE

Broken people inevitably break those around them. No matter the situation that led you to begin the process of forgiveness, it's more than likely that the situation involved a very broken person. How do you know that person was broken? By looking at the affect he or she had on you. Did you leave the relationship whole? Or did you leave broken, now in need of repair yourself?

1 Timothy 5:24-25 sheds light on this cycle beautifully. *"The sins of some are obvious, reaching the place of judgment ahead of them; the sins of others trail behind them. In the same way, good deeds are obvious, and even those that are not obvious cannot remain hidden forever."* Many of us give a loud "Amen!" to the first part of that verse. The sins of some people in our lives are blatantly obvious. But if we look ahead to the next part that says "the sins of others trail behind them," we see that some sins are a little more gray and difficult to recognize. This describes the cycle of broken people perfectly. One obviously broken person has sins that are readily on display, thus causing the victim to be very aware of what was done to them. However, if not healed, the victim continues the cycle of sin and leaves a trail of brokenness behind him or herself as well. The second person never

sets out to hurt others but is usually just trying to survive with what has been left broken inside of them.

As I reflect over the broken years of my own life, the closer I get to the years of intense suffering, the uglier the picture and more revealing the truth. I was a broken wreck of a person, and my pattern of behavior showed it. I was too young at the time to see it for what it was, but now when I look back, I am so humbled and saddened by my behavior. I was trying to do everything I could to ease my pain. I was trying so hard to replace the pieces that had been taken from me.

I had experienced abuse by men both physically and sexually. In my later relationships with men, my truly shattered state became evident. Because of what I had gone through, I was very confused about sexuality. I sped recklessly along, trying to make sense of it all, not even thinking for one second about what I was doing to the other people involved in my life. I was acting out of a response to something that had happened to me. I had wounds that were so deep that, without realizing it, I was trying to self-medicate. And, remarkably, it seemed to work for a while. It boosted my confidence, validated my being worthy, made me feel pretty, loved, and secure. But, these feelings were temporary. Inevitably, they faded as I moved on, wondering why my relationships were ending so badly.

What puzzled me during this process of relationship-jumping was the trail of hurting people I left behind. I figured they were weak or simply didn't understand what adult relationships were like. When, in reality, they had entered the relationship as whole people (mostly) and left broken. In my poor attempt to repair my own broken state, I carelessly broke everyone around me. Now, did I realize this at the time? Of course not. Had I realized, I never would've behaved the way I did. But, you see, as the product of abuse, I was a broken person myself. The abusers in my past were clearly broken individuals as well, and they had left me in the same state. As I look back now, I recognize my actions toward the men I dated as very similar to the actions of the men in my past. While I was selfishly trying to repair myself, these men were falling in love with me. Imagine their heartache when, out of nowhere, I up and abandoned each one to move on to someone else. I can imagine that pain because that is the exact pain I experienced through one of my broken relationships. Yet, somehow during this process, that truth had never occurred to me.

Because I am now healed, graciously pieced back together by the Lord, I can see the trail of sin left behind me. My heart breaks for those I hurt, and I feel sorrow for the wounded shell of a person I once was. All I was trying to do was to survive. I wanted my life to go back to normal. That's the human desire, right? But, sadly, when I aimed at fixing myself, I missed the mark completely. "I" should never have been figured into the solution. Who was I to think I could actually repair my broken self? According to the Word, there is only one person with that job description, and it isn't me and, my friend, it isn't you either! Isaiah 53:5 says, *"But he [Jesus] was pierced for our transgressions, he was crushed for our iniquities; the punishment that brought us peace was on him, and by his wounds we are healed."* Jesus was crucified for our sins so that we could be healed. And not just physical healing, but emotional healing as well. He is the only one who can restore what has been broken. No matter how hard we try in our own strength to repair ourselves, we are incapable of being our own physician. Other than Jesus, no one has the ability to restore himself or another person back to wholeness. A human being may make improvements; surface adjustments may be apparent. However, without the healing touch of Jesus, being restored back to complete wholeness and having more peace, more joy, and more contentment than before the brokenness occurred just doesn't happen. I've tried; it simply isn't possible.

When I finally came to grips with the humbling reality that I couldn't fix myself or my heart or my past, it was amazing how quickly I began to see the path to healing stretched out before me. And, at the start, was forgiveness. How precious and tender and gracious the Lord was to me. How patient He still is with me! He gently guided me down the path of healing—and guess what! It didn't include a bunch of self-help books, hobbies, or frivolous spending (and believe me, I had tried all of those). No, I was healed through the forgiveness, love, grace, and mercy of Christ Jesus. I can confidently stand before you today and say my heart is whole again. I am truly able to love and to accept love in return. But, it would never have been possible without surrendering my life, my hurt, and my brokenness to Jesus Christ.

My friend, it is a process. I would encourage you to begin by asking the Lord to reveal to you your "trail of sin" that follows after you wherever you go. First and foremost, you must confess your sins to the Lord. Ask him to show you areas of your life in which you may need to repent. He is ready and waiting to forgive you and begin rebuilding your life, but he will not force change on you. You must take this first step. Once this has been done, you may need to consider asking forgiveness from those you have hurt. It is humbling and not easy to do, but rest assured that each time you take a step towards repentance and restoration, grace will meet you half way. My prayer for you is that your asking of forgiveness will help those you have hurt begin their own healing process. If they don't heal, the risk of the cycle continuing is high. Make a vow to be one less. One less broken person breaking other people. You are now in Christ and have been made whole again! His mercies are new every morning. Trust the Lord to be faithful to complete the work begun in YOU!

The second part of 1 Timothy 5:24-25 says, *"In the same way, good deeds are obvious, and even those that are not obvious cannot remain hidden forever."* When we surrender our broken pieces to the Lord, he will be faithful to heal us and begin transforming our lives into something new. Our "trail of sin behind us" shifts into good deeds that become apparent to everyone around us. And, even the parts that are not obvious can't stay out of sight for long! The Lord longs to use your restored broken pieces to bring himself glory and put his mighty work of healing on display! Amen!

One of the first things I had to do was surround myself with others who were "whole." 1 Corinthians 15:33 says, *"Do not be misled. Bad company corrupts good character."* Take notice of who your friends surround themselves with and who you, in turn, surround yourself with. You need to keep your guard up to keep your character in tact. If you see things in your friends that do not line up with the Word of God, and you continue to stay around them, your character will be threatened, and you risk ending up in another broken situation.

Whether you realize it or not, others are watching you, and your behavior could affect theirs. Proverbs 22:1 says, *"A good name is more desirable than riches; to be esteemed is better than silver or gold."* The Lord desires to bring himself glory through YOU; it is difficult to do that when you are running around acting foolish or hanging out with other foolish characters! Let your name be a testimony to who you are in Christ. Let your behavior shout praise to your Savior who redeemed you out of the pit! You are to desire a good name, which the Lord will give you when you fully submit yourself to him. How? When Christ becomes the center of your life, you will begin acting like him. When brought before the governor to be crucified, his accusers could find nothing of which to accuse him. Why? Because his life was a picture of love, healing, forgiveness, mercy, grace, and truth. He had a good name, and his life glorified the Father. Like Jesus, your name should inevitably speak of the One who gave you a new one.

The Word of God tells us that when we become a son or daughter of God, he gives us a new name. I love how this is displayed through the story of Abraham. Genesis 17:1-8 reads, *"When Abram was ninety-nine years old, the LORD appeared to him and said, 'I am God Almighty; walk before me faithfully and be blameless. Then I will make my covenant between me and you and will greatly increase your numbers.' Abram fell face down, and God said to him, 'As for me, this is my covenant with you: You will be the father of many nations. No longer will you be called Abram; your name will be Abraham, for I have made you a father of many nations. I will make you very fruitful; I will make nations of you, and kings will come from you. I will establish my covenant as an everlasting covenant between me and you and your*

descendants after you for the generations to come, to be your God and the
God of your descendants after you. The whole land of Canaan, where you
now reside as a foreigner, I will give as an everlasting possession to you and
your descendants after you; and I will be their God."'

Notice how the Lord entered into this situation describing himself—he declared who he was, the Lord, "God Almighty." Make no mistake, when the Lord shows up in your life, He will make himself known! He then gave Abram a command to walk before him "faithfully" and to be "blameless."

When we walk faithfully with the Lord through obedience to his Word and by listening to the quiet voice of the Holy Spirit, we already begin taking on a new name. We become like Jesus, who was blameless. Praise the Lord!

At this command, Abram fell face down, which was an act of complete surrender. By his actions, he was taking a humble, servant-like position, declaring that he knew God was who he said he was and that Abram himself was God's servant. This is where God made his covenant with Abraham, calling him the "father of many nations." To fully grasp this covenant God offered, it is important that we understand Abraham's situation. He did not have any sons by his wife at that time. And, given that he was nearly one hundred years old and his wife ninety, this would seem nearly, if not completely, impossible. Let this be an encouragement to you, that once God makes himself known in your life, and you are walking faithfully and blamelessly with him in Christ Jesus, nothing is impossible. I believe the Lord takes a particular liking to using our "impossible" situations to bring him glory. He makes beauty from ashes; he places the simple among princes. He likes doing what only He can do—the miraculous.

After the Lord shared with Abram what he was going to do through him, he gave Abram a new name. But he didn't stop there! He didn't just give him any new name. No, he gave him a new name *with* a promise! God declared that the covenant he made with Abraham came with an inheritance for all of the descendants who would come after him, promising that it would be an "everlasting covenant" with his children and that he would be their God. He then threw in an added bonus! The Lord decided, as well, to give him possession of the very land in which Abraham had been residing as an outsider.

Now, the Word of God tells us that we have a new covenant through Christ Jesus. When he died on the cross for us, the old covenant disappeared. Hebrews 8:6, "*But in fact the ministry Jesus has received is as superior to theirs as the covenant of which he is mediator is superior to the old one, since the new covenant is established on better promises.*" God sent his Son to be our Mediator before the throne, thus making himself accessible to all of us! He loved his people so much that he wanted a relationship with all of us. And, he said that this one comes with even better promises! Hebrews 8:10-12 tells of the new covenant that God made with his people: "*This is the covenant I will establish with the people of Israel after that time, declares the Lord. I will put my laws in their minds and write them on their hearts. I will be their God, and they will be my people. No longer will they teach their neighbor, or say to one another, 'Know the Lord,' because they will all know me, from the least of them to the greatest. For I will forgive their wickedness and will remember their sins no more.*" We don't have to wait like Abraham did for God to "show up." Under the new covenant we have in Christ Jesus, we can go directly to him!

But, even though many of us have accepted Christ as our Lord and Savior, due to past hurts and brokenness in our lives, we have stopped identifying with him. We carry around our "old" names or the labels that others have given us along the way, thus continuing the cycle of brokenness. My friend, you are not defined by your past. You are not defined by your past or even present behavior! If you are a child of God, then your identity rests in Christ Jesus. You belong to him, and your old name is gone. Paul states this wonderfully in 2 Corinthians 5:16-17. *"So from now on we regard no one from a worldly point of view. Though we once regarded Christ in this way, we do so no longer. Therefore, if anyone is in Christ, the new creation has come: The old has gone, the new is here!"*

My friend, there are no boundaries to God's goodness towards his people. There are no obstacles that He cannot overcome, and no situation that he cannot change. It all begins by falling on your face in complete surrender—just like Abraham—and accepting your new name. The old you is gone, and the new you is here! Though broken people have affected you, your new name and newness in Christ bear the key to break their hold on you. And, that key is forgiveness.

Your Journey. . .

1. Ask the Lord to show you areas of your life in which you need to repent. What did he bring to mind?

2. Prayerfully consider those whom you may need to ask for forgiveness.

3. List the people whom you primarily surround yourself with.

4. Do their lives honor God? If so, list the areas you see as glorifying to God.

5. What parts of their lives are not bringing glory to God? How have you noticed these areas affecting your life? If needed, ask the Lord to bring people into your life who will strengthen you in your walk with the Lord.

6. What "labels" have been put on you by others from your past?

7. Ask the Lord to show you who you are in Christ and what your new name is. Journal your thoughts here.

FORGIVENESS

Chapter 6

FORGIVENESS

I imagine this chapter is one you may have been dreading or antici-
pating. Most of us understand the basic concept of forgiveness. At
one point or another in your childhood, you may have been taught
to simply recite the phrases "I'm sorry" or "I forgive you" after an
argument with a playmate. Being taught to apologize and to accept
apologies lays a valuable foundation in a child's social development.
However, I fear that as adults, we still cling to our child-like view
of apologies as something said without deeper meaning.

In one of my favorite passages of Matthew 6, Jesus teaches us
how to pray by giving us The Lord's Prayer. The last few lines
say, *"Forgive us our debts as we also have forgiven our debtors"* (Matthew
6:12). Then Jesus brings the prayer to a close. He follows The Lord's
Prayer with one final note regarding forgiveness. I find it interesting that Jesus did not choose to further explain any other segment
of The Lord's Prayer other than the segment on forgiveness. He
seemed to know that we would innately ask the question, "why?"
Why would we want to forgive others when we pray? He simply
answers the unasked question. Matthew 6:14-15 says, *"For if you
forgive other people when they sin against you, your heavenly Father will*

also forgive you. But if you do not forgive others their sins, your Father will not forgive your sins." If there was any doubt as to the importance of forgiveness, it was clearly removed in this final note.

So, the heaviness of unforgiveness has been revealed. By choosing to hold onto an offense, refusing to forgive the one who has committed an offense against us, we prohibit our Heavenly Father from forgiving us. Scripture is clear on this subject. I don't know about you, but for me the idea of anything separating me from my Heavenly Father is sobering. Yet, how many times have we stumbled over a situation in which someone has repeatedly hurt us? Our instincts are not to forgive. We say, "Okay, the first offense was difficult enough to forgive, but I did it. Now, am I seriously expected to *continue* forgiving this person???" Some wounds are so deep and go so far back that it would take the length of a football field to list them all. I get that. By no means do I negate the severity of wounds that have left you emotionally—perhaps even physically—scarred.

I believe Peter was as incredulous about the issue of forgiveness as we are. He posed this question to Jesus. *"Lord, how many times shall I forgive my brother or sister who sins against me? Up to seven times?"* Jesus answered, *"I tell you, not seven times, but seventy-seven times"* (Matthew 18:21-22). I appreciate Peter's honesty in asking Jesus this question; without it, we would be left with some gray areas on this issue. Jesus was direct in His response; he made it clear that it is imperative for us to continue to forgive—not just once, but as many times as it takes.

Why do you think Jesus was so persistent about this issue? I believe it's because forgiveness is the heart of the gospel. Christ's primary purpose in coming to earth was to die in our place so that we could be forgiven. But, I would also propose to you that forgiveness doesn't solely benefit the receiver; if it's done the way Scripture defines it, we will discover there is a gift for the giver as well. A gift that I believe far outweighs any benefit given to the receiver: freedom. By walking through forgiveness (and not just the beginning stages, but completely following it through to completion), you enter into true freedom—freedom from the bondage in which your offender placed you. You see, forgiveness is not an option; it is the key that sets you free! It is one of the main elements in Christ's message of setting the captives free and releasing those in "darkness."

Personally, my darkest days were the ones in which I lived bound by the wounds of my past—unable to break free, repeatedly running into the same issues, time after time. I was blaming those who had wronged me, holding on to my hurt and allowing current offenses to add to the bloody pile of past wounds. For many of us, this is how we have lived. Not because we have deliberately chosen to, but because we felt imprisoned by our experiences. News flash: We don't have to live like this! Christ came to set us free—not just from the bondage of our own sin, but from the bondage of the sin of others. And, as painful as it may sound at first, forgiveness is at the heart of it.

So, what does it look like to forgive? Do I just say "I forgive you" and poof! It's done? As Scripture tells us, we can do and say many things, but the Lord looks at our hearts. Forgiveness is a heart matter. Webster's defines the word *forgive* this way: "To cease to feel resentment against, on account of wrong committed. To give up resentment or claim to requital on account of (an offense or wrong); to remit the penalty of; to pardon."

I love that it uses the word *feel* because we can easily claim to forgive someone, yet as soon as we are around them, our insides turn and we begin to feel anything but forgiveness. So, how do you know if you've truly forgiven someone? Try this test: When you think about or see that person, is there an absence of dislike, anger, or hurt? When good things come to that person, are you genuinely glad for him or her? If so, then you know you have truly forgiven. However, if, when you see that person, something begins to tug on your insides as you remember everything they ever did or said to you that was wrong or hurtful, or you just get plain uncomfortable and don't know why, you still harbor unforgiveness in your heart. You may find yourself angry, envious, or resentful if they have something better than you. These are all signs that you have not completely forgiven them. Now more often than not, our initial step of forgiveness isn't an act stemming from feelings or emotions—it is a matter of obedience. While our feelings are an excellent indicator of our heart, the beginning of the forgiveness process is pure obedience *apart* from feelings.

Now, I realize this isn't a popular way of looking at forgiveness, nor is it comfortable. But, what if I told you that it is possible to truly forgive in the way described above? You can actually forgive someone who has wronged you once, and even those who have deeply wounded you repeatedly. It is possible!

So where do we begin? We first have to start with the offense—or multiple offenses. I would encourage you to take a moment and ask the Lord to reveal to you those whom you need to forgive. It may be one person; it may be several. Take some time now to list each offense or hurt as it comes to mind, using a separate sheet of paper for each individual. Some offenses may be small, while others may be larger and more painful to remember. By writing each one down, you acknowledge the place of importance they have had in your life. You are giving them validity as discussed in the first chapter. As Christians, we don't always allow ourselves the right to admit that we've been hurt. We get so caught up in striving to please the Lord that when we are hurt, we quickly bury the offense as if forgiven. We act like it doesn't hurt us because we think it shouldn't. The truth of the matter is, if it still hurts, it means we haven't forgiven the offense. That is not at all the heart of Christ. He was sent to "heal the brokenhearted." How can he do that if we are pretending not to be heartbroken? You must first allow yourself to hurt before you can begin to forgive.

As you list each offense or hurt, allow yourself to be angry. Just as David offered his brokenness as a sacrifice, allow yourself to be broken. Allow yourself to feel every emotion that pops to the surface when you read that offense. By doing this, my friend, you are allowing yourself to become what you are—human. You are woundable. You are breakable. You are meant to feel even when it is painful. This is why we need a Savior: because in our own humanness, we are unable to heal the amount of pain that some wounds have inflicted on us. We can cope; yes. But, we don't have to simply cope! We can be healed; we can be set free.

With deeper wounds, as you begin allowing yourself to feel anger over the wrong committed, you will most likely feel a sense of grief—sadness over the injustice that was inflicted upon you. I encourage you to press into that sadness and allow yourself to grieve.

Upon your grieving, invite the Holy Spirit to comfort you. One by one, lay each hurt at Jesus' feet and ask him to heal you.

Now, there may be some items on those lists that do not evoke any emotion at all. Usually, those are some of our deepest hurts. It could be that those wounds have been buried so deeply that the raw emotion they originally brought with them is no longer near the surface. That's okay. Ask the Lord to help you grieve those hurts. This may be a process. I would encourage you to keep those pieces of paper near you in your daily time with the Lord. Continue to ask the Lord to help you grieve those hurts, and eventually the emotion will come to the surface. Once it comes, don't be surprised if the grief is overwhelming. I had never even cried about some of my deepest hurts. When they eventually came to the surface, I was hit hard. But, sweet friend, don't be afraid. The Lord will meet you there. He was with you in the past, and He will be with you now. There is freedom waiting for you. Press in and allow the healing to begin.

Some of you may be thinking, "Wow. That is a lot of work for one simple hurt!" I agree. The initial "session" of sitting down and processing the offenses of your past and present may take a little longer than you'd like. But, the good news is that you only have to do this initial "list" once. You are going through years of wrongs that have been done to you, finally giving them a voice and putting them in their proper place: out in the open where forgiveness can begin. Once this has been done, you are no longer working with past issues but are focused on the present. Look at it like this: if I were a tennis player and injured my knee, my tennis game would falter. If I made the choice to push through the pain and keep playing, my knee would undoubtedly struggle to function in every game and over time would become a serious problem. If years later I finally decided to go see the doctor for help with my injured knee, my treatment would probably involve surgery followed up by therapy to get my knee back to normal. Now, had I immediately upon injury gone directly to the doctor, the regimen of recovery would have been significantly less, and my knee would have healed much faster.

The same is true of the issues we are dealing with in this chapter. You are now going through "surgery" on your past wounds. This may take a little time. But once this is dealt with, your next offense will be much easier to handle. You will go through the same steps, but they will be at the onset of the hurt and not years later, thus making the recovery time much faster.

To give you an example, just the other day someone said something that really hurt me. My motives behind a specific parenting decision were questioned. As any parent knows, criticism of your parenting skills jabs at your heart no matter who it comes from. Given that the decisions I make for my children are made through prayer and are based on the foundations laid out in Scripture, you might think this particular attack wouldn't bother me, but it hit me hard. Knowing that this certain individual uses tactics like that to manipulate others into getting what this one wants, I recognized it and set my boundaries accordingly. However, it still hurt. The words, no matter how you slice them, still stung. The old me would've pulled myself together, shrugged, and swallowed the hurt, forcing myself not to think about it or let it get to me. Then, the next time something similar happened, the injury would go deeper because it was building on top of the old wound. And on and on it would go. But, I have learned how to deal with the hurt since then. Now, I identify the hurt. I give it a name. I allow myself to be mad. I sit myself down, give it to the Lord, and ask him to heal my heart. I then make the choice to forgive. Done.

All of that takes me approximately fifteen minutes from start to finish; then, it is over. I can talk about the offense without feeling sad or mad. I can look at the individual with forgiving eyes because I have been set free from the hurt that person had tried to inflict on me. I can even look at that person with love. I say this not to boast but to encourage you! If someone like me can get to this place, so can you.

So, once we face the hurts, allow ourselves to be angry, and give our hearts to the Lord for healing, what comes next? We make a choice. We choose either to begin to forgive or not to forgive. God can't force you to forgive someone, and neither can I. But, for your heart's sake, I pray you make the choice to forgive.

Jesus gives us a painful yet beautiful example of making this choice. Jesus knew the pain of betrayal personally. Judas, one of Jesus' disciples and closest friends, betrayed him by accepting payment from the Roman soldiers for leading them straight to Jesus. Judas knew why they wanted to find Jesus; they wanted him killed. *That* is a serious betrayal. After Jesus was arrested, Luke 22:64-65 tells us that *"the men who were guarding him began mocking him and beating him. They screamed 'Prophesy! Who hit you?' and, they said many other insulting things to him."* Jesus was then brought before the people, who were given a choice, and they chose to see him crucified. Crucifixion is an extreme form of torture and one of the most brutal ways to die. Jesus was beaten until he was nearly unrecognizable. His head had thorns pressed into it. He had nails pounded through his flesh to attach him to a cross. As if this wasn't enough, there were people taking pleasure in his pain. In Matthew 27:30-31, it describes that during Jesus' crucifixion, he was mocked and spit on. While he hung on the cross dying, some of the soldiers were making bets and dividing his clothes among themselves. This man was tortured physically, emotionally, and mentally to an extent that is nearly impossible for most of us to comprehend. Yet, in Luke 23:34 we read this passage, *"Jesus said, 'Father, forgive them, for they do not know what they are doing."* Few of Jesus' words during his crucifixion were recorded, and I find it incredible that after being abused, mocked, beaten, humiliated, and in unbearable physical pain, he found the strength to speak those words. He could have kept quiet, enduring the torture and focusing all of his energy on completing his earthly assignment. Instead, He not only found the physical ability to speak, but out of his heart came forgiveness.

Many parts of the crucifixion story may relate to our lives. How many of us have been betrayed by close friends who did exactly what they knew would hurt us the most? Jesus felt this with Judas. How many of us have been abused physically or emotionally? Jesus endured ruthless abuse by the soldiers during his arrest and crucifixion. How many of us have been completely humiliated as others watched and enjoyed the show? While dying on the cross, Jesus experienced all of this while enduring brutal suffering.

Like it or not, on some level, all of us can relate. I am humbled deeply at this revelation: how many times have I selfishly clung to my anger over betrayal, hurts, and abuse? The most piercing hurt of all was when the abuser seemed to take pleasure from my pain. That to me was unforgivable. Yet, Jesus experienced all of this on a magnified level and still he forgave—not after he died and was resurrected, not after he was in heaven with his Father. No, he forgave in the moment. He chose to forgive the instant the hurt was inflicted.

I encourage you to read Luke 23 and allow the weight of Jesus' suffering to penetrate your heart. He was human; he felt every emotion and every physical pain inflicted on him. But, he is also the Son of God. And, He chose to bear that torture, abuse, humiliation, and death *as a human* so that *you* could receive forgiveness. As Ephesians 1:7-8 tells us, *"In him we have redemption through his blood, the forgiveness of sins, in accordance with the riches of God's grace that he lavished on us."* Thus, because we have been forgiven, sin no longer separates us from our Heavenly Father. And if we believe that Jesus is the Son of God, confess our sin with our mouths, and ask for forgiveness, it will not only be given to us, but we will be saved. *"For God so loved the world that he gave his one and only Son, that whoever believes in him shall not perish but have eternal life. For God did not send his Son into the world to condemn the world, but to save the world through him"* (John 3:16-17).

As recipients of this grace and unwarranted forgiveness from our own sin, we have no option but to forgive in turn. Just as you and I have found freedom through what Christ did for us on the cross, there is immense freedom in extending that grace to others. And this grace begins with love…

Your Journey. . .

1. When you think about those who have hurt you, do you feel dislike, anger, or hurt? When they are blessed or prosperous, are you genuinely happy for them? Or, do you immediately remember the list of every hurtful thing they did to you? Do you feel uncomfortable when you're around them?

2. Take a moment and ask the Lord to reveal to you those whom you need to forgive. Write down each name and begin to list each offense or hurt as it comes to mind.

3. Look over your list for a moment. Just as we learned that David offered his brokenness as a sacrifice, allow yourself to be broken. Allow yourself to feel every emotion that rises to the surface as you ponder each offense. *(Press into your emotions and allow yourself to be angry and to grieve. Upon your grieving, invite the Holy Spirit to bring you comfort. One by one, lay each hurt at Jesus' feet and ask him to heal you.)*

4. Are there grievances on your list that do not evoke any emotion at all—ones to which you respond coldly? Ask the Lord to help you grieve over those hurts. Write these down on a piece of paper; keep it near you in your daily time with the Lord. Continue to ask the Lord to help you to express true grief over those hurts.

5. In reading about Jesus' suffering in Luke 23, how were you affected? Were there any parts you could relate to?

Chapter 7

THE GREATEST OF THESE IS LOVE

And now these three remain: faith, hope and love.
*But the **greatest of these is love** (1 Corinthians 13:13).*

As Christians, we often forget that the greatest of these is love—not sermons, not rules or commandments—just love. To love a broken, hurting person is to get a glimpse into the heart of God. Love opens doors that sermons cannot. Love tears down walls that arrogance, pride, and legalism have built up. Love is it. Love is the key that unlocks doors into lives that have been otherwise plagued by abuse, deceit, broken promises, addiction, and betrayal. As beautiful as this word "love" is, Scripture does not use it lightly.

*But I tell you, **love your enemies** and pray for*
those who persecute you (Matthew 5:44).

*But to you who are listening I say: **Love your enemies**,*
do good to those who hate you (Luke 6:27).

*But **love your enemies**, do good to them, and lend to them*
*without expecting to get anything back. Then **your** reward*
will be great, and you will be children of the Most High,
because he is kind to the ungrateful and wicked (Luke 6:35).

When I read those passages and allowed the heaviness of their truth to sink into my heart, I was uncomfortable. Not only because I didn't like what I was reading but also because I realized that I had been doing the very opposite of what Scripture had commanded me to do. I was immensely challenged by this concept of showing love to those who had hurt me. It seemed impossible, but I was too intrigued to just pass over it. If this was stressed so much in Scripture, there had to be a reason. I decided to experiment and give this concept merit in my life.

Before we can love, we first must understand what love is and what love isn't. Scripture defines love in 1 Corinthians 13:4–8. *"Love is patient, love is kind. It does not envy, it does not boast, it is not proud. It is not rude, it is not self-seeking, it is not easily angered, it keeps no record of wrongs. Love does not delight in evil, but rejoices with the truth. It always protects, always trusts, always hopes, always perseveres. Love never fails."*

In all honesty, this isn't easy to do with my spouse whom I love dearly, let alone my enemies! Now, you may be thinking, "Well, lucky for me, the person who abused or hurt me is no longer in my life. I get a free pass on this one. Woo hoo!" Before you flip to the next chapter, consider this: On one level or another, all of us are forced to face "enemies" to whom we need show forgiveness and love in our daily lives … *daily.* I say this tongue-in-cheek because if we are honest, each of us knows someone who has a way of getting under our skin. For some of you, however, you may be dealing with someone regularly who weighs on your heart much heavier than just a surface annoyance. It may be the very person we have been discussing in this book: someone who has betrayed you or violated your trust on a deeper level. This may be a family member you are obligated to see repeatedly, forcing you to try to cope with the situation; it may be a co-worker or even a friend. I know what that's like. This is the situation I found myself in and that in many ways inspired this book and specifically this chapter.

Even if you aren't dealing daily with the person who betrayed or injured you, it's nonetheless likely that certain people in your current circle seem compelled to pour salt in the wounds your betrayer left. But, what I am about to share with you is vital to your freedom. This was difficult to work through. In many ways, it not only hurt my heart but also my pride. However, I am now certain that without this step, I would not have been set free from my past, and without it, you will never be free from your past.

Love your enemies. I was challenged by this principle not only with one of my betrayers whom I encounter on a regular basis but also by the little daily annoyances of people who remind me of that person. One person in particular had an amazing way of adding fuel to the flames of pain. Somehow this person managed to ignore or misconstrue my every word. Even my best intentions were somehow turned on me. Every time I was around this person, their unspoken mission seemed to be to completely pick me apart and grind up the pieces. It was exhausting to fight what felt like a losing battle. In my frustration, I finally came to a place where I was forced to ask God to show me what to do because nothing I had tried was working, and I was failing miserably. This is when I came across these principles in Scripture. At first, I did not want to hear them! But the Lord spoke to my heart, revealing through his Word that I needed to show this person love. But, what do you do when you don't feel love towards that person? How do you show someone love when you utterly despise them?

Matthew 5:44 says, *"Love your enemies **and** pray for those who persecute you"*

I started with prayer. Reluctant at first, I began to pray for that person. In praying, I asked God to change my heart and to allow me to begin feeling His love for that person. I asked God to allow me to see that individual from God's perspective. Some kind of action is usually required in forgiveness. At first, these actions can be uncomfortable and at times very humbling. But, I can promise you that the results and benefits far outweigh the temporary discomfort. Little by little, it became easier, and my prayers slowly evolved. "Lord, help this person to not be mean" soon became "Father, bless this person. Bring your favor into their life, and I pray that they would be surrounded by your love. Show me how to love this person and how to be a blessing." Each day, I prayed, and each day my heart began to move away from despising and closer towards loving that individual.

I did this for about a year. I don't know whether it was noticed or not, but I'm sure my countenance began to change around that person. No longer was I walking on egg shells, wondering what might be said or done next. I was quietly confident. Without that person's knowledge, I was looking for ways to express God's love. Fear no longer plagued me when I was in that one's presence. Instead, I eagerly awaited any opportunity to show love.

One might think that this would have softened such an individual but, on the contrary, it seemed to fan the flames of anger and make that person more determined than ever to destroy me. As Proverbs 25:22 says, *"In doing this, you will heap burning coals on his head, and the LORD will reward you."* Perhaps my kindnesses stung a little? Completely unprompted, this person would make the most condescending remarks at every opportunity. It became painfully obvious that this particular individual was looking for a fight. Proverbs 12:16 also says, *"A fool shows his annoyance at once, but a prudent man overlooks an insult."* This was probably one of the most difficult verses to put into practice. Everything in me wanted to think of a clever "comeback" to this person's remarks. My mind was so tempted to ponder all of the things I "should've said."

Yet, the Lord continued to impress upon me his admonition to "love them." Love always, always, always includes humility. And, where humility is present, pride is absent. Unknowingly, I had embarked on a crash course of overcoming my pride and embracing humility. I think the hardest thing about demonstrating kindness was that I was forced to swallow my pride. In order for me to truly display Christ's love, I had to be genuine. A sticky sweet, contrived response would have completely defeated the purpose. No, this had to be real. This had to be genuine love and for that love to be genuine, I had to love the way Christ did. I had to become the servant. I had to say no to myself and every ounce of my pride. I had to turn the other cheek. I had to put the other's needs above my own...even if that one was my enemy. I had to choose to speak life instead of death. I had to love those who persecuted me... really, really love them. I had to be the hands and feet of Jesus to those who hated me and plotted against me. This concept took some getting used to, but instead of fighting it, I embraced it. It came down to a simple choice, and I chose Christ's way instead of my own. From that moment on, I can honestly say that after every remark and sly comment this person threw at me, I truthfully acted as though they hadn't said it and chose to respond kindly. There were instances when what was said cut so deeply that it took all my strength to keep silent. There were also times I had to bite my lip and walk away. But, I always refused to fight back.

Months went by, and I assumed that things with this person had quieted down. Then I learned of a stream of hateful lies this person was spreading about me and my family. One might argue that at this point, I should've given up my mission and thrown the entire love idea out the window; I could have washed my hands of it and decided that although Scripture said to love an enemy, it didn't really apply to my situation because it was clearly making things worse. Then the Lord brought to mind Luke 6:27. *"Love your enemies; do good to those who hate you."* The word "hate" seemed just as strong as the word love. I truly felt *hated*. I think there comes a time in our walk with Christ where we are forced to embrace the challenge; where we have to draw the line through mediocrity and cling to our faith; and where we become so focused on Jesus that we die to self to become more like Him. This was that turning point for me. I could've followed my human impulse. I could have confronted that hateful individual and exhausted myself attempting to prove that those accusations against me were false. I could've let it eat away at me and keep me tossing and turning all night, trying to devise a plan to clear my name. Or, I could choose to walk by faith and trust the Word of God to lead me. Proverbs 12:23 says, *"A prudent man keeps his knowledge to himself, but the heart of fools blurts out folly."* I decided to take God's Word and put it to the test. I did not respond to this person's attacks or act as if I knew about it. Through prayer, I felt that, in this situation, it wasn't my job to clear my name or sort through the truth and the lies; I was to trust the Lord to do that. Instead, I needed to focus on the Lord's command to love that person.

Shortly after this incident, I learned that one of that person's loved ones had passed away. Given the transformation my heart had already experienced, my heart deeply ached out of a sincere place of love. And, out of that place came my opportunity to display Christ's love.

With every attack on your life or your character, the Lord always presents an opportunity to bring Himself glory through you. Once you begin to focus on glorifying Christ, the focus shifts away from you and on to how you can reach out to others.

I saw my opportunity, and I seized it. I mailed this person a card expressing my condolences and included a gift card to a favorite store. Later as I was shopping, I saw a shirt of one of this person's favorite sports teams. I picked one up and gave it to that person the next time we met. I could've passed it and walked on by, but something in me again seized an opportunity to show love.

Although seemingly insignificant, these small acts of kindness slowly began to change me. As Luke 6:35 says, *"But **love your enemies**, do good to them, and lend to them without expecting to get anything back. Then your reward will be great, and you will be children of the Most High, because he is kind to the ungrateful and wicked."*

I may never know whether or not my actions were received in love. But what I do know is that I am exactly where the Lord wants me to be, loving those who persecute me, giving without expecting anything in return, and forgiving even if it means doing it daily. Who knows what this person thinks about me? Honestly, I've given up caring. The only opinion that matters is God's opinion. His is the only one I am interested in, and if he loves that other person, then—through Christ—so can I.

Love can also be displayed in speaking truth. As Ephesians 4:15 says, *"Instead, speaking the truth **in love**, we will grow to become in every respect the mature body of him who is the head, that is, Christ."* Though difficult, sometimes Christ's love calls you to love someone enough to speak the truth. There have been times in my life where, honestly, it would've been easier to ignore an offense, forgive silently, and simply move on. Yet, out of my love, I had to share the truth regarding someone's words or actions and the resulting effects. This forces you to be honest and completely transparent, which when you've been hurt is the last thing you want! However, the Lord challenged me specifically in Ephesians 4:25; *"Therefore each of you must put off falsehood and **speak truthfully** to your neighbor."* To put off falsehood means to stop pretending something is one thing when it is clearly another. In some situations, the Lord may lead you to speak truthfully to someone who has hurt you. Not out of anger or spite, but as Ephesians 4:15 said, out of *love*.

Christ loves us enough to show us the truth in our own lives; at times, the truth isn't comfortable. As His followers, we must be willing to speak the truth, even when exposing that truth is uncomfortable. Love isn't easy—it may lead you to walk away from a ready fight or, conversely, to confront an issue head on when it would be easier to just look the other way. Through the guidance of the Word of God and prayer, in surrendering each situation to Him, He will be faithful to direct your steps. He will gently guide you through loving your enemies in every circumstance. Through my personal experience, I have found that, when dealing with those who have hurt me, my display of love will usually involve a combination of both turning the other cheek and speaking truth. The key to both is that they each be rooted firmly in love.

Of course, applying the Lord's command toward someone who has abused or violated you will, of necessity, be different. Your safety is of utmost importance. Forgiveness and love will come—but not at the expense of putting yourself in harm's way. Before you can ever show Christ's love to others, you must first accept His love for you. He desires your freedom and safety. You are his temple, and if anyone is harming you, that is not okay. You are free to forgive from a distance.

Please hear me when I say that if you are still involved with or in contact with someone who is or has been abusive, or if you feel threatened, please contact a pastor, counselor, or the police. You need to get help in order to remove yourself from that situation.

Sweet friend, there is no shame in Christ Jesus, and removing yourself from harm is a must.

Many of us face challenging enemies—such as abusers—from our pasts. I address this cautiously because I don't want anyone to get the impression that putting yourself back into the life of someone who has abused you is what God requires of you. That is not what Scripture is saying, and I would never counsel you to do that. When you are dealing with an abuser, strong boundaries must be in place. Once you have removed yourself from the abusive situation and have begun the process of grieving, healing, and forgiving, love—God's holy love—will come. I don't say this lightly; I know firsthand about the lingering anger, fear, and control that can haunt your life even after the abuse ends. But, having walked through this and having allowed Christ to heal me, I am no longer bound by my abuser. I am free.

I got to this place from working through the steps I shared earlier. The same principle applies. It may look different, but it is the same principle. I started by praying for that abusive one. It was *not* easy. I will not sugarcoat it or pretend it was something that it wasn't. It was hard. But, grace met me, and in time, it became easier. Through prayer, my heart changed and softened. The anger subsided and the feeling of wanting to destroy that person the way they had destroyed me also left. You might ask, "What on earth did you pray for? What *could* you pray for someone like that?" I started simply by asking God to help me *want* to pray for that individual. That was honestly my prayer for months. It was all I could do, so that was what I did.

Eventually, my prayers evolved into praying that my former abuser would find Jesus. That God would seek that one out and heal that one of whatever wounds had been inflicted that resulted in such abusive behavior toward me. I now pray that this person can eventually find the freedom that I have found. *This* is how I love that person. Let me be clear, I do *not* send my former abuser cards or buy t-shirts to share. My boundaries remain quite firm. However, praying for that one is something I can do while keeping my boundaries and safety intact.

What showing love to your enemies will look like for you is something that the Lord will reveal to you through prayer and wise counsel. Ask the Lord to reveal your enemies to you. Maybe some are present in your life today; maybe some are haunting you from your past. Maybe you're like me and get the "pleasure" of both. I encourage you to sit down and make a list of these individuals and stick it in your Bible or post it on your wall with a sticky note. Put it where you will be reminded to pray. Ask a good friend or a mentor to hold you accountable in prayer. You, my friends, will be richly blessed and will find such great freedom in doing this.

We read in 2 Corinthians 1:8-10 that *"We were under great pressure far beyond our ability to endure, so that we despaired even of life. Indeed in our hearts we felt the sentence of death.* **But this happened that we might not rely on ourselves but on God,** *who raises the dead. He* **has** *delivered us from such peril, and he* **will** *deliver us. On Him, we have set our hope that He will continue to deliver us, as you help us by your prayers."*

Your Journey. . .

1. Ask the Lord to reveal your enemies to you. Make a list and put it somewhere that will remind you to pray for them. Ask a good friend or a mentor to hold you accountable in prayer.

2. Commit Matthew 5:44 to memory. ("Love your enemies *and pray for those who persecute you."*)

3. Ask the Lord to reveal to you what showing love to your enemies should look like. Write your thoughts here.

4. In what ways are you encouraged by 2 Corinthians 1:8–10?

Chapter 8

GET UP AND WALK

Forgiveness is an amazing gift—and amazingly, I am finding it to be more a gift for the giver than the receiver. It takes away someone's ability to have power over you. Their old tricks of manipulation and control vanish—not because they are different but because you are walking in love and forgiveness. When you begin walking in kindness, regardless of their behavior, they're at a loss for what to do or how to respond. Choosing love instead of hate, choosing to be kind and gracious instead of being stubborn and rude, choosing to speak encouraging words instead of sitting in silence—all of these are changes in YOU. Not changes in them.

Once we submit to this way of thinking, God begins to do an incredible work in our hearts and lives. When I began changing my behavior, at times I didn't even recognize myself. And through this, God began calling me to rise above the person I used to be. I would become convicted in simple conversations that weren't God-honoring. Normally, I wouldn't have given it a thought, but when you begin living your life in submission to God, it automatically affects everything else. God begins to refine you—and not always in the big things. He often starts with the small ones. This is where life-changing transformations begin. For me it was in forgiveness, kindness, and self-control. These were the areas of my heart that needed serious adjustments.

When you surrender your hurts and losses to the Lord, the ability to pray for your enemies and display genuine love through your interactions will supernaturally begin to happen. As you embark on this journey, I pray that you begin to experience this change. Shifting your perspective on how you view those who hurt you makes such a huge difference. You begin seeing them with compassion rather than fear. You begin to show them mercy rather than anger. You begin walking in victory instead of defeat.

When we live as broken people, we inevitably live crippled, wounded lives. Once we have surrendered our brokenness to the Lord and invited him to begin the healing and restoration process, it is time to get up, stretch our legs, and start walking. Jesus displays this principle in John 5. While visiting Jerusalem, he came to a pool where many of the sick, blind, lame, and paralyzed would gather. One specific man caught Jesus' attention, a man who had been an invalid for thirty-eight years. Jesus approached him and in verses 6-8, we read the following conversation:

[Jesus] asked him, "Do you want to get well?" "Sir," the invalid replied, "I have no one to help me into the pool when the water is stirred. While I am trying to get in, someone else goes down ahead of me." Then Jesus said to him, "Get up! Pick up your mat and walk." At once the man was cured; he picked up his mat and walked.

How true is this today? So many of us choose to live sitting as invalids, when all that is needed is for us to get up and walk out our healing. Jesus has come to set us free. We have learned of his desire to restore us and heal us. Once we believe this and accept this, it is time for us to get moving. I pray that you are already putting into practice everything we've learned thus far: praying for your enemies, loving your enemies, and choosing to forgive your enemies. But, one final step that is necessary to fully walk out your healing is to take responsibility. Now, we are not responsible for our reactions to the abuse or neglect we may have experienced as children. The responsibility I'm referring to is our adult responsibility.

As adults, we are responsible for our own behavior—regardless of the circumstances that surround it. In many situations, especially in the areas of intimate relationships, when the guns start firing, they are usually firing in both directions. If both parties were to be honest, typically they will admit to allowing their anger and resentment to build to such a level that both say things that they shouldn't have said and do things they shouldn't have done. The result is a broken relationship where both are in need of not only forgiving each other but also being forgiven as well—thus putting them at a 50/50 stand still. Both are equally wrong, yet out of stubbornness, they will hold up the other's faults and refuse to admit an ounce of wrong-doing on their own. Yet, there are other situations, especially in the areas of betrayal or broken trust, where one party is initially one hundred percent at fault, but the other party, out of hurt and anger, reacts poorly to the offense. When working through forgiveness, even if the other party was ninety-nine percent at fault, you are still responsible for your one percent—even if it was merely reactionary.

God began to impress this on my heart a few years ago. I will admit, when he first began challenging me on this, I thought, "you want me to do *WHAT*?" I couldn't believe what he was asking me to do, nor did I like the idea. But, the deeper I allowed myself to fall into this line of thought, what I began to realize was mind-blowing: who was at fault no longer mattered. No matter how terrible the other's behavior had been, in this case, I still needed to ask forgiveness for my reaction to it. Now, just to clarify, by no means in doing this was I making their list of "wrongs" right. Those were not my responsibility; they were theirs. I am only responsible for me; though I could go on and on about how my behavior was only in response to their choices and make light of my actions, at the end of the day they were still my actions. That person didn't make me do anything. I made the choice to respond out of hurt and anger rather than out of a Christ-like spirit, and I had to take ownership of those actions. It didn't matter whether that person was living right or not; sin is sin—sin that needed to not only be confessed to God but also confessed to the one I had sinned against.

Again, I cannot stress to you enough how much I didn't want to do this! This was taking my trust and relationship with the Lord to an entirely new level. He pushed me to completely lose all sight of everyone else's behavior, to forget how wrong they were, and to focus my attention solely on my actions and how they lined up with who God wanted me to be. This was not only totally foreign to me but also immensely frightening. By embracing this, I would surrender all control of the situation. That was one thing I did not want to do. My hands were locked together, trying to prove the other's fault and plead my innocence. I didn't want to let go. However, God's Word is true, and I couldn't ignore the weight of it. As uncomfortable as it was at first, instead of shying away from its truth, I did the opposite; I pressed into it. By this point I had learned not to fight God; it simply isn't worth it. Deep down, I knew his way was right, and even though it didn't make complete sense yet, for the first time I was willing to go in blindly and trust him. I was amazed at the safety I found there. Fully resting in the truth of God's Word has a comfort level that is unmatched elsewhere. The peace you find in knowing that you are submitting your will and mind to God's Word brings a comfort unmatched elsewhere. Time and time again, I am humbled by the consistency of this truth.

In reading this, the Lord may be shining light in a specific, dark area in your life. You may not know how to even begin processing the idea of going to that person and admitting your fault, asking for forgiveness. That idea alone is extremely humbling and utterly terrifying! Our fear stems from not knowing how that person will respond; knowing that in your own strength, you may not be able to handle what is said or done in return. We might all say that baring one's heart and soul and making oneself vulnerable to an enemy doesn't make sense. And, yet, that is precisely why we need the Lord. In our own strength there is absolutely no way we could go through with it, not to mention doing it while maintaining a good attitude and saying everything that needs to be said. It goes against our human nature—which is exactly why the Lord wants us to do it. Not to humiliate us or to open up our wounds and have salt poured in them, but to glorify himself through our pain. In walking out the heart and soul of forgiveness the way Christ designed it to be, we become a light in an otherwise very dark place. And that is how he is glorified! By taking the first step out of the land of rejection and starting to walk into the arms of redemption, you can trust that Jesus will be more than faithful to carry you through, all the while displaying his beautiful craftsmanship as your healed heart is exposed.

I don't know what your walk will look like. Only you and the Lord know the areas of your heart where unforgiveness has been present and what walking that out will look like. What I do know is that if you ask him, he will show you. He takes such delight in presenting his restored children to this world as a platform to his goodness and glory. Rest assured that this is one part of the journey that you do not want to miss! As you begin seeking the Lord about how he wants you to begin walking out your forgiveness, I encourage you to meditate on the following verses from Psalm 34:

> *I sought the Lord and He answered me; he*
> *delivered me from all my fears.*
> *Those who look to Him are radiant; their faces*
> *are never covered with shame (verses 4-5).*
>
> *No one will be condemned who takes refuge in Him (verse 22).*

As I was beginning to embrace my need for responsibility, this particular passage seemed to jump off the page. When we are facing places of our past that we don't want to see, shame wants to sweep in and bury us. After that, fear comes rushing in to cover our mouths and keep us in hiding. But, God's Word promises He will deliver us from our fears! This is for you! You don't have to be afraid. Your face is radiant and not covered with shame. Not because you are perfect, but because you're forgiven! You don't have to be ashamed of what you did or of what's been done to you. There is no condemnation for those who are in Christ Jesus, and that includes you!! In verse 22, we are reminded again that if we take refuge in him, we will not be condemned! Verse 19 says, *"A righteous man may have many troubles, but the Lord delivers him from them all."*

This is so comforting as it reassures us that it's okay to have many troubles. Having troubles doesn't mean that there is anything wrong with you or that you have necessarily done anything to provoke them. Godly people don't have perfect lives; the difference between us and the world is that God delivers us from our troubles! And, not just some—ALL. Now think about verses 17-18:

> *The righteous cry out and the Lord hears*
> *them... He is close to the brokenhearted*
> *and saves the crushed in spirit.*

In order to fully walk this thing out, you must be completely honest with yourself about what you believe. Begin confessing with your mouth the truth of the Scriptures. You have to believe that when you cry out to God, he hears you. You have to believe that he was and is close to your broken heart and will rescue you when your spirit has been crushed. Be encouraged that the Lord not only sees and hears you, he also desires to rescue you. You have to make a choice before you begin walking out your forgiveness. Choose to take refuge in the Lord, trusting that you will not be condemned. All desire for "control" must be laid aside as you take refuge only in the Lord and nothing else—not even yourself.

Once the Lord reveals to you those whom you need to ask for forgiveness, sit down and ask him to help you write a list of everything you need to include. One item that may need to be included is "delayed forgiveness." As we learned earlier, Scripture says we are to forgive immediately. By holding on to any offense, we are sinning. As much as the idea of writing down all of these things may originally horrify you, I promise that as you begin writing each line, an immense amount of freedom will begin to take place in your spirit. As you write each line, confess each sin to the Lord. Repent and lay it at his feet. Once you lay them at the feet of Jesus, these burdens are no longer yours to carry; He immediately forgives you, freeing you from the bondage of your own actions. This, in turn, releases you to forgive the actions of the other person, setting you free completely!

As I mentioned earlier, the Lord challenged me specifically in this area. I clung to Psalm 34, sought the Lord fervently, and eventually arrived at the time for me to walk it out. I met the individual for coffee. With shaking hands, I held my list and read each line with a trembling voice. And, I may be wrong, but I think the one to whom I spoke was shaking too; the "coffee date"/confession and apology was totally unexpected and shocking, I am sure! When I was done, the individual thanked me and seemed genuinely appreciative. However, I did not meet with this person seeking any particular action or response. I did what I felt God wanted me to do; His approval was the only one I was looking for.

As Ecclesiastes 7:8-9 says, *"The end of a matter is better than the beginning."* That couldn't have been more true at the end of that day. There was an immense amount of closure for me as I left that coffee shop. No, I did not receive any explanations regarding that individual's past actions, nor did I receive any apologies from that person. But, somehow, that didn't matter. I was free from it all. I was free from what had been done to me. Honestly, free. That day, the power shifted. I was no longer afraid of that person. Dread at the possibility of seeing that individual vanished. Anxiety about unexpectedly running into that one disappeared. My vision had changed. It's like someone had taken away smudged glasses and had replaced them with new, clear ones. Now I can look at that person without seeing my laundry list of every wrong done to me. I see an old friend whom I genuinely cared for; I began to see that person through the eyes of Christ, and as scary as that may sound, it didn't feel scary at all. In front of me stood a broken human being—someone who had deep wounds that had been hidden. Someone who possibly, in many ways, had been wronged in much the same way as that one had wronged me. I saw someone in need of the healing I was now experiencing. This is the key; this is the secret to how the fullness of forgiveness works. This is God's desire for all of us: that we can live our lives free from the burdens, hurts, and injuries that cripple us and leave very little room for the Holy Spirit to move. This is your ticket to wholeness.

As you allow the weight of this chapter to sink in, I encourage you to seek the Lord in prayer. We are all called to walk out forgiveness; I realize it may seem like an overwhelming task, but all it takes is one step in the right direction. Ask the Lord to show you what that next step is. Ask him for the grace to enable you to do it. Below is a portion from my prayer journal as I was struggling with the heaviness of beginning my own walk. Perhaps this will help you get started.

"Oh Father, please hear me! I am trying to be obedient to you by walking out forgiveness. Lord, I surrender this to you. I trust you to give me the strength to do what I know you've asked me to do. Let me be a light in a dark place. Give me eyes to see them the way you see them. Be there to guide me just as you have done before. Please, Father, deliver me from my fear."

Your Journey. . .

1. Ask the Lord to show you what "walking out forgiveness" should look like for you and journal your thoughts.

2. Be really honest with yourself about what you believe. Consider Psalm 34:17-18 (*"The righteous cry out and the Lord hears them...He is close to the brokenhearted and saves the crushed in spirit"*). *Do you believe this to be true?*

3. Have you taken refuge in the Lord, or in yourself by attempting to "control" your situation?

4. From which individuals do you believe the Lord would have you seek forgiveness?

5. With the Lord's help, list everything you need to include. (*Do you need to include "delayed forgiveness"?*)

6. As you process each line, confess each sin to the Lord. Repent and lay it at his feet.

Chapter 9

FEAR VS. FAITH

Fear is the ultimate opponent to loving those who persecute you. Fear can be crippling, which is why it is so powerful. You may be afraid of an individual's reactions if you turn the other cheek or respond in kindness rather than with an insult. You might fear that by acting in love, that fearsome one will hate you even more and intentionally hurt you; or that you will somehow be attacked or taken advantage of. Fear is the enemy of love. After all, love in its purest form is *fearless*. Just look at what Christ did for us on the cross. He selflessly offered the ultimate sacrifice— his own death! He looked fear straight in the eye and triumphed victoriously! Fear is the definitive challenge to overcome when learning to love your enemies.

Fear is also one of the major opponents to truly leaving our past behind us and walking into the lives the Lord has called us to live. A few years ago, I came to a realization about myself and about God, some of which was comforting, some discouraging. Yet, all were true, and the truth resonated with a peace that I otherwise would not have had. I realized that when everything I could do in my own strength (physically, mentally, and emotionally) was taken away, I retreated. I would mentally lock myself away, hunker down, and wait until the coast was clear before coming out again. I wouldn't pray or run to God for help. Instead I would retreat and hide like a human hermit crab. I was forced to ask myself, "Why do I keep doing this?" Up until that point, I truly had believed that I had an unmovable relationship with God. I prayed without ceasing, read the Bible, and listened for Him to speak to me, but now the reality of my inconsistent behavior rocked my very foundation.

Romans 8:35 says, *"Who shall separate us from the love of Christ? Shall trouble or hardship or persecution or famine or nakedness or danger or sword?"*

In some odd way, I had come to believe that because of what was going on around me, either God didn't love me the way He used to, or He no longer found me worthy of that love. I had a very difficult time admitting this to myself, but it was true. At my core, this was what I believed.

However, Romans 8:37-39 goes on to say, *"Now in all these things we are more than conquerors through Him who loved us. For I am convinced that neither death nor life, neither angels nor demons, neither the present nor the future, nor any powers, neither height nor depth, nor anything else in all creation will be able to separate us from the love of God."*

In order for me to continue clinging to my former belief that God's love was questionable, I would inevitably have to denounce the above Scripture: it was contrary to what I had adapted as truth. I was forced to confront the solid truth of God's Word because obviously, up until this point, I had believed a lie. My personal truth pertaining to God's love towards me had, in fact, been false.

The reality was that I was afraid. I was living in fear to the point of doubting my Heavenly Father's love for me. When you have dealt with betrayal of any kind, your ability to trust becomes severely skewed. Yes, I trusted God, but like my trust on earth, my ability to believe in His unwavering love for me now had limitations. What I once found secure, was now shakable. My life's experiences were dulling my perspective of my God and had placed perimeters around his love for me. Yet, I desperately wanted to believe that nothing could separate me from the love of Christ Jesus, as Romans 8 described.

I truly believe that no matter our environment, circumstances, or how much our ability to trust has been abused, we all want to believe this. Yet, the enemy has hindered so many of us from walking out of our personal prisons due to our inability to fully embrace this. Why? Because, if we were one hundred percent certain that Romans 8:37-39 was true, then we wouldn't be afraid of anything! We would be immovable powerhouses able to walk triumphantly through any obstacle course that this life could set in front of us. Imagine how life would be if you were convinced that you had more than enough strength and ability to overcome any situation. The truth is, when we fully surrender our lives (every ounce of who we are and have been) to Christ, we enable him to operate through us with supernatural strength and ability. God's Word says that in him, we are not afraid of death, this life, any spiritual forces, what lies ahead in the future, or what has been haunting us from the past. Through the highs of this life and even in the darkest valleys, we are confident that Christ's love for us is powerful enough to overcome anything and carry us through. When we fully embrace who God is, what he has done for us, and just HOW much he loves us, fear begins to move out of our hearts, and a new resident begins to take its place: faith.

At this point, we know that your trust in humans has failed. You have learned that people on this earth will let you down and at times hurt you. You can either live in fear of more people doing the same to you and fear that God has abandoned you as well, or you could choose to live in faith. You could choose to have faith that all of God's promises in his Word are true. Not just some—but all.

God's Word is filled with promises for us. They are little light bulbs of truth that have the power to shine in very dark circumstances. These promises were given to us when we became sons and daughters of God. Scripture is filled with them! God's Word is truth, and all of the forces of this world cannot argue with God's Word. So, when we speak God's Word into our circumstances, the situation has no option but to yield to God's Word. Sadly, I feel we have forgotten the power of God's Word and fail to use a gift that is rightfully ours to use.

The Lord loves it when we include Scriptures in our prayers. We not only can use them when we petition our requests to God, but we also can use them to rebuke the enemy when our minds are bombarded with fearful thoughts. When we are reminded of our past or when insecurities flood our souls, we have promises to cling to. When we are being attacked by someone who has betrayed, abused, or hurt us, we have promises to deliver us. God's Word is filled with promises for His people to stand on.

I am going to get a bit personal with you and share how this has worked in my life. Years after the abuse had ended, I found myself the focus of my former abuser's attention. Although no longer part of my everyday life, this person was part of a much bigger circle— my family. No matter what lengths I took to remove myself from the abuser's destructive behavior, I still felt trapped. This person would seek out ways to engage me in conflict or arguments; I became increasingly frustrated—until I realized a liberating fact: this person had an insatiable need to control. And not just to control me, but to control anything and everything that was in this individual's life. No matter who it affected or how ridiculously small the situation was, like most abusers, this one *had* to be in control. I found myself avoiding any type of conflict; it was simply too exhausting! I never could figure out how to combat someone so bent on deception and manipulation. To that individual, it was a game, and it was a game I was unwilling to play. Therefore, I would just assume the role of the player who always forfeited. I bowed out of every argument and let that one "win" as much as possible.

I hated the whole situation, and I hated myself for being so afraid. I was stuck. I had forgiven and had even come to a place of loving that person, but dealing with repeated confrontations was something I didn't know how to handle. How should I stand up for myself and yet still demonstrate God's love? How could I go about my life without being afraid of unpleasant reactions?

That was when faith began to take root in my soul. I had to let God handle my battles and let Scripture take over in my prayers and thought life. This is critical not only to your personal deliverance but to a serious breakthrough in your situation. There is no better illustration of this than when Jesus was tempted by Satan in the wilderness. Matthew 4:1-4 says, *"Then Jesus was led by the Spirit into the wilderness to be tempted by the devil. After fasting forty days and forty nights, he was hungry. The tempter came to him and said, 'If you are the Son of God, tell these stones to become bread.' Jesus answered, 'It is written: "Man shall not live on bread alone, but on every word that comes from the mouth of God."'"*

Verse two tells us that Jesus was hungry. The enemy immediately hit him with a challenge that played on his body's need for food. The enemy isn't any different today than he was then. He will come at you with his weapons aimed at your most vulnerable areas and at your weakest moments. That is how he worked then, and that is how he works today.

Notice Jesus' response: "It is written," and then he quoted a Scripture that put Satan right in his place. We know that Jesus was hungry, so it is safe to assume that the idea of turning stones into bread probably seemed appealing. I have to believe that his flesh was struggling with his spirit at this moment; his flesh and body wanted nourishment. Yet, instead of giving in or even entertaining the idea, he combated his flesh with what he knew to be true: the Word of God. The enemy doesn't like to bring attention to himself, or his schemes would be too obvious. But, if he can shift our attention onto ourselves—onto what feels good at the time—he has a better chance of getting us to leave the path God has planned for us. I don't think when Jesus spoke this verse that it was just for the enemy's benefit; I believe he was speaking it to himself as well. He was commanding his spirit to override his flesh and everything his body and mind were telling him to do.

Let's continue in verses 5-7:

"Then the devil took him to the holy city and had him stand on the high-est point of the temple. 'If you are the Son of God,' he said, 'throw yourself down. For it is written:

"'He will command his angels concerning you,

   and they will lift you up in their hands,

      so that you will not strike your foot against a stone.'"

Jesus answered him, 'It is also written: "Do not put the Lord your God to the test."'

Notice that in both situations, the enemy started his proposi-tions with the same word: "If." This is another indicator of a tactic the enemy likes to use and is still using today. He shifts our atten-tion away from what he is doing and causes us to question what we know to be truth. How many times do we begin pedaling down the path to fear all because we paused and listened to a thought that began with "if"?

Yet, again, look at how Jesus responded: "It is written…" He immediately responds with Scripture. Notice, also, what he didn't do; not once did he answer the enemy's "If" question. Satan di-rectly questioned his position as the son of God. Jesus very well could have spent a good amount of time and energy defending his position in His Father's kingdom. I can't help but ask myself why he didn't do this. There may be many reasons, but I believe one reason was because Satan already knew the answer. The question had nothing to do with Satan trying to decide if Jesus was who he said he was—he knew who Jesus was. His motive was purely to distract Jesus with an argument that wasn't necessary. If he could get Jesus to engage him, he had a shot at trying to convince him to go against what the Father had commanded him to do—or if nothing else, exhaust him in the process, depleting his energy, and possibly delaying his mission.

Another reason I believe Jesus didn't respond is because it was an attack on who Jesus was. If Jesus had been concerned with his "status" or with what the people on this earth thought of him (like many of us are), that part of his heart would've immediately responded out of fear of being questioned on a subject that already had him concerned. Instead, we see by his response that Jesus was not concerned about himself at all—his ONLY focus was God the Father. He didn't care what others thought about him—he knew his right standing with God the Father, and therefore that question didn't merit a response. It is paramount to our deliverance that we stay focused on the Lord and not on ourselves. If we remain grounded in who we are in Christ and keep our eyes fixed on the plan God has for us, then we will not fall into the enemy's "trap." Proverbs 4:23-26 says, *"Fix your gaze directly before you... only take ways that are firm."* Jesus, knowing the tactics of the enemy, only responded with the Word of God, as should we.

Now, let's look at how their meeting concluded. I love this next part! Continuing on in verses 8-11, we read:

> *"Again, the devil took him to a very high mountain and showed him all the kingdoms of the world and their splendor. 'All this I will give you,' he said, 'if you will bow down and worship me.' Jesus said to him, 'Away from me, Satan! For it is written: "Worship the Lord your God, and serve him only."' Then the devil left him, and angels came and attended him."*

Again, same ol' tricks. The enemy is playing on Jesus' flesh and tempting him with things he doesn't have, followed by another "if." Now, in our everyday lives, we are not directly conversing with the enemy as Jesus was here. Yet, if we stay alert as Scripture commands, we will be able to see how this same line of attack is prevalent in our day-to-day experiences…specifically in our line of thinking.

How many times do we find ourselves looking at things we don't have and wishing they were ours? How often do we do this not just with material things but with people? All it takes is one moment of pause, one moment to begin thinking that maybe we are missing out on something better, for the enemy to swoop in and give us the ultimate "if": *if you bow down and worship me, all of this will be yours.* This right here is when Satan shows his cards. Turning you away from God is his ultimate goal, and he will use every trick he has to try and get you to this definitive question. How on guard we must be in our minds!

I can't stress enough the importance of keeping your mind focused on God; we do this by hiding the Word of God in our hearts. *"I have hidden your word in my heart that I might not sin against you"* (Psalm 119:11). Jesus says in Matthew 12:34, *"For the mouth speaks what the heart is full of."* And, here Jesus beautifully displayed what was hiding in his heart; the Word of God. Jesus responds with Scripture, quickly rebuking the enemy at the same time, thus ending the conversation instantly. Notice how the two go hand in hand. When you rebuke the enemy, using the God's Word as your weapon of choice is vital.

Why is it so powerful? Hebrews 6:18-19 says it perfectly: *"It is impossible for God to lie, we who have fled to take hold of the hope set before*

us may be greatly encouraged. We have this hope as an anchor for the soul,
firm and secure.”

God's Word is the ultimate truth. Satan is no match for the
power the Word of God holds. It is impossible for God to lie, which
is why we can take stock in the promises of his Word. This verse is
very personal to my journey. Try reading it with this spin on it and
see if it doesn't resonate in the same way for you. "it is impossible for
God to lie (so I don't have to be afraid that he won't come through
for me), we who have fled (leaving fear, unforgiveness, anger, hurt,
and pain behind) take hold of the hope set before us (God's promises) may be greatly encouraged. We have this hope (promise) as
an anchor for the soul (emotions of fear, loneliness, heartache, loss)
firm and secure (unmoving and safe).”

I encourage you to commit this verse to memory and hold tightly
to it. When you feel the flood of fear, anger, hurt, loneliness, or loss
beginning to rush into your soul, speak this truth with your mouth.
When the "If" questions begin to bombard your mind (which they
inevitably will do, so prepare ahead of time!), tell your flesh what
the truth is, just as Jesus did. Hide this verse in your heart so when
faced with temptations, your mouth will speak God's truth.

Your Journey. . .

1. In light of your circumstances, what has your personal truth pertaining to God's love toward you been?

2. How has your life's experiences jaded your perspective of God and his love for you?

3. What three critical points stood out to you in Jesus' dealings with Satan in the wilderness?

4. What are some "If's" that the enemy has used on you in the past? Have you found yourself looking at things you don't have and wishing they were yours? Have you done this not just with material things but with people?

5. How have you combated the "If's" in the past? Have you hidden God's Word in your heart?

6. Explain how Hebrews 6:18-19 has affected you. (*"It is impossible for God to lie, we who have fled to take hold of the hope set before us may be greatly encouraged. We have this hope as an anchor for the soul, firm and secure."*)

7. Write this verse down where you will see it daily and commit to memorizing it.

Chapter 10

WHEN THE DAY COMES

Earlier, I mentioned my fear when faced with a confrontation from a past abuser. It has been a difficult journey on which to embark, but what I am about to share with you completely changed my life. This truth is not only paramount in dealing with someone who once had power over you, but this can and should be applied to nearly every situation in which you need a breakthrough, whether personal or relational.

Ephesians 6:12 says, *"For our struggle is not against flesh and blood, but against the rulers, against the authorities, against the powers of this dark world and against the spiritual forces of evil in the heavenly realms."*

1 Corinthians 10:3-5 continues with the same line of thought. *"For though we live in the world, we do not wage war as the world does. The weapons we fight with are not the weapons of the world. On the contrary, they have divine power to demolish strongholds. We demolish arguments and every pretension that sets itself up against the knowledge of God, and we take captive every thought to make it obedient to Christ."*

Ephesians tells us that our struggle is not with people, but against the spiritual forces of evil. Then, 1 Corinthians tells us that we do not fight this battle or struggle with the weapons that we would normally think to use. On the contrary, the weapons we should use have the power to demolish spiritual forces of darkness (not people). And, not only that, but they have the authority to demolish arguments and every pretension that sets itself up against the knowledge of Christ.

Do you understand what is being said? Whatever battle you face right now, whether internally or with another person, this battle is not really of the physical realm. The real fight is in the spiritual realm, with the enemy's forces and their attack against YOU. We learned in the previous chapter some of the ways the enemy tries to attack us—he can attack our minds through our thoughts or use other people's words or actions. And, remember what his ultimate goal is: He wants you to shift your focus away from God's plan for your life and onto yourself, thus giving in to the temptation to worship *him*.

I want you to take a moment and reflect on your current situation(s) and analyze how the enemy has attacked you, whether in your mind or through others. Has he gotten you to put your focus solely on yourself and away from God? If not, have you possibly started down that path of "Ifs"? Are you living in fear in this situation or in faith? How have you tried to fight this battle so far? Have you been fighting in the natural or in the spiritual? What weapons have you been using? Are you anxious or at peace? Oftentimes, we don't see the *real* fight until we begin looking for it. Once you see the real battle, it is much easier to begin fighting it proactively with faith.

Continuing in Ephesians, we learn how to fight this battle with the weapons GOD has given to us. Not the weapons of the world or of our flesh.

In Ephesians 6:13-17, we read, *"Therefore put on the full armor of God, so that **when the day of evil comes**, you may be able to stand your ground, and after you have done everything, to stand. Stand firm then, with the belt of truth buckled around your waist, with the breastplate of righteousness in place, and with your feet fitted with the readiness that comes from the gospel of peace. In addition to all this, take up the shield of faith, with which you can extinguish all the flaming arrows of the evil one. Take the helmet of salvation and the sword of the Spirit, which is the word of God."*

Now, if you're like me, you've read these verses many times, not fully comprehending what this looks like when put into practice. When I think about this verse, I see my little brother at age five, dressed up as a "soldier for the Lord" at Halloween, proudly wearing his "Armor of God" to our church harvest party! It's easy to take lightly the things that we have either heard repetitively over time or things that we do not fully understand. Let's break this down piece by piece and allow the Lord to show us how to use these real weapons in the battles we are facing.

Verse 13 references "when the day of evil comes;" for all of us, that is any day when we are tempted, whether in thought or by the actions of others, to step outside the boundaries that God has laid for us. It says to prepare for that day by putting on the full armor of God, so that when we are attacked, we will be able to stand our ground. I don't know about you, but for me, that was HUGE. If there was one thing from which I was very ready to be set free, it was being bound to other people's behaviors and their affects on me. Being able to stand my ground with unmovable faith, in spite of what others may say or do, was a life-changing event for me.

Verses 14-17 tell us to stand firm with all of the components of the "armor" of God, the first one being the "belt of truth." I once heard a lyric in a song that really resonated with me. It said, "Teach me to speak truth in love and humility." I loved that line. It's amazing how difficult that actually is to do. Rarely do we confront people in love, let alone in humility. When we speak the truth, it must come from a deep-rooted place of humility. Otherwise, the person to whom we are speaking will be unable to relate to us.

So often I have been the pained recipient of a self-righteous platform speech from one very pious person attempting to reach out to one very broken person. Rarely does this ever work to bring about the desired result. More often than not, the broken person leaves feeling more ashamed, hurt, and bruised, as well as less hopeful than they were to begin with. I have been on the receiving end of this form of attack and looking back, it left nothing but a bitter taste in my mouth. Was that pious person's heart in the right place? Probably. Did that make their words hurt any less? Absolutely not. Now, looking back through newly-healed eyes, I am able to see it clearly for what it was. However, at the time, it was nothing more than a stab at my already bleeding and broken heart.

Remember, 1 Corinthians tells us that our weapons give us the power to "demolish arguments." I believe that comes from speaking truth that is rooted in love and humility. When we focus on the truth, we are cutting out the excess that really doesn't matter. We are guarding our tongues, abstaining from foolish talk—truth typically is stated with few words. There is such wisdom and protection in doing this. With the truth buckled tightly around us, we have the power to demolish arguments because arguments ignite emotions—not facts. When focused on speaking the truth in love and humility, we can repel any verbal attack that comes our way.

I love the breastplate of righteousness because it covers our hearts. Keeping a righteous heart is so essential to our success in any spiritual battle. Scripture tells us that we can pursue righteousness by detesting and fleeing all things that are evil. Keeping our hearts holy, pure, and in right standing with God comes from a constant place of repentance and a willingness to be humble before the Lord. Habitually asking the Lord to reveal any sin that our hearts harbor is of utmost importance in leading a righteous life.

Fitting our feet with the readiness that comes from the gospel of peace is an interesting one to me. For some reason, this piece of holy armor didn't strike me as part of a battle strategy. Readiness, I get. We need to be constantly ready/prepared for a spiritual battle. The peace part was what left me feeling perplexed. Then I read that being ready *comes from* the gospel of peace. Scripture tells us that there is a peace that passes all understanding. I didn't fully understand this concept until the last few years. When trials come and the storms of life begin to rage, most of us don't react by being immediately at peace. Worry, fear, and anxiety are more readily apparent when faced with alarming situations. Yet, as followers of Christ, there is a peace that passes all understanding. In the midst of tragedy, we can remain steadfast and calm. It is this peace that readies our feet for battle. There is no better warrior than one who in the heat of the battle remains in control of his wits. He is fearless and therefore continually ready for whatever may come. This happens when a heart is fully reliant on the Lord for *everything*. When you come to a place where you know that if absolutely everything you loved was taken from you, you would be okay because you had the Lord—that is where you discover the peace that passes ALL understanding. That peace will ready you for any battle, and you won't be afraid of the outcome.

Verse 16 continues by saying, *"In addition to all this, take up the shield of faith, with which you can extinguish all the flaming arrows of the evil one."* It is faith in the Word of God: believing what it says about YOU and God's promises over your life. You will defend yourself against every thought of fear and insecurity with faith in God's Word. Standing behind God's promises will protect you from every arrow the enemy can shoot at you.

Concluding with verse 17, we read, *"Take the helmet of salvation and the sword of the Spirit, which is the word of God."* Putting on the helmet of salvation is knowing what you've been saved from and who you belong to. When we forget our need for a Savior, we quickly become an open target for the enemy. Remembering what the Lord delivered you out of and what he did for you on the cross is critical. Following that up with the Word of God as your sword is powerful. This is what we saw earlier when Jesus was in the desert. He fought his battle with the Word of God—period.

But, what does that look like? How do you know what Scriptures to use? I don't know your particular situation, nor do I know the extent of the battle that you are facing. But, one thing I do know is the power of the Holy Spirit when we devote time to reading God's Word. Come before the Lord in prayer and ask Him to move his

Holy Spirit to direct you to the Scriptures you need in your tool belt. Come with expectation, and he will deliver!

Matthew 7:7 says, *"Ask and it will be given to you; seek and you will find; knock and the door will be opened to you."*

Stand on that Scripture when you come before the Lord, and expect him to answer. When he begins speaking to you through his Word, revealing Scriptures for you to use, memorize them. That way, when your day comes, you will not only stand your ground in faith, but you will combat the enemy and send him running!

It is imperative that we stay continually alert and prepared. As much as I'd like to tell you that whatever trial you are currently facing or whatever past hurt you are healing from will be your last, I can't. Once you move on from this situation, you will undoubtedly come up against another mountain, and it may be similar to the one you are facing today, or it may be completely different. Why am I so sure of this? Because we cannot control the behavior of other people. I cannot force a wayward spouse to stay faithful to me, I cannot make a friend stay loyal, nor can I keep my boss from firing me—all of that is out of my control. What *is* within my control is my response to their actions and how I allow them to affect me. I don't say this to discourage you; I say this so that you will utilize what we have learned, hiding God's Word in your heart to prepare for the next set of trials that come. If you are not fully prepared, you will most likely end up flat on your back on the battlefield.

My "day" came just this past year. My dear husband Zac and I have been married for a while now; together we have two children, and I have felt the security of a faith-based marriage and home. It has been such a blessing being married to someone who is not only my husband but also my best friend. Then, I learned that he had been quietly struggling in an area that my first husband had struggled in, which was one of the many reasons for our divorce. You can imagine my devastation as an old wound was instantly ripped open and what felt like a heap of salt was poured into it. I was stunned. The world that I thought I had known to be solid, became unsteady. My immediate reaction was familiar. I ran to our bedroom and grabbed a suitcase; I wanted to run away. I refused to feel that pain again! Yet, just as quickly as I had reached for that suitcase, the Lord quietly captured my attention. He reminded me of who I was now; I was not the same person I was the first time around. This time, I knew what was true about me and what was true about my God.

I set my suitcase down and looked at the man I loved and whispered through tears, "I'm not going to leave." I went upstairs into the bathroom and locked the door behind me. What happened next, I must tell you was very strange. Quite honestly, I don't know how else to say this except that I didn't recognize myself or what came out of my mouth. I sat in the bathroom and began crying out to God. I thanked him for his mercy. I declared over and over again his faithfulness and goodness. I began speaking truth because somewhere inside, my spirit knew the lies that the enemy would begin hitting me with; it knew that if I sat still for even one minute, those lies would have the victory over me. I was not going to let that happen to me again. I would not allow the enemy to rob me of my joy this time. I knew who I was fighting, and I met him head on.

I spoke to the enemy these words, "You took my first marriage, you have tried to attack nearly every relationship I've had, and now you're trying to take this marriage too. FINE! You can try to take everything there is from me, but one thing you CANNOT take from me is my right to praise MY God. You cannot take away my ability to praise Him. He is a good God! He is a faithful God, and He is stronger and more powerful than anything you could ever try to do. He will deliver me, and He will prosper me through this! This IS THE DAY that the Lord has made, and I WILL REJOICE AND BE GLAD IN IT!"

When I got up, I looked in the mirror. I did not see a broken person whose world had just been shaken. I saw a strong woman of God who knew at the core of her being that no matter what happened to her in this life, her God would be faithful to see her through it. This person was someone I had never seen before. For weeks afterwards, I waited for the sorrow and insecurities to creep into my heart, but they never did. I kept thinking, "Why am I joyful? This is really strange!" I was not happy with my circumstance; but I was joyful because I knew I was in the Lord's hands. No matter what the outcome was, I knew I would be okay because I knew the strength and character of my God. That is freedom. For me, that was the moment I could step back and take a deep breath, knowing that all the work the Lord had been doing in me through repenting, forgiving, loving, and choosing to stand on faith had finally borne fruit. I didn't feel the chains from my past any longer; the prison door had been thrown open, and I was walking out.

Having shared that with you, I want you to know that the Lord has used my husband's struggle for so much good—not only in him, but in our marriage; the list of praises that has come out of that situation is too long to count! And, my husband will tell you that part of the reason we are where we are today is because of my reaction to his behavior. I chose to stand on the truth of God's Word instead of what my emotions and past were telling me to believe. In doing that, healing and restoration were able to come much more quickly. I've shared this with you to give you a glimpse of what the other side of forgiveness and healing can look like. When you've experienced healing and restoration through God's grace, there is a transformation that takes place at the core of your being. You become fearless. You are not afraid of any outside circumstance because you are solely secure in the provision and safety of the Lord. This is a picture of *continual restoration*. This is freedom.

Everything we have covered so far on this journey worked together and resulted in my restored wholeness. But, I did not embark on this road by myself. Ecclesiastes 4:12 says, *"Though one may be overpowered, two can defend themselves. A cord of three strands is not quickly broken."* With the Lord on your side, along with at least one other believer, you can move mountains. I have had strong women of God alongside me through this entire process. They held me accountable. These precious friends loved me enough to point me back in the right direction when I started heading down the wrong path. Without them, this process wouldn't have been impossible, but it would have been much harder. I would encourage you to begin this battle by putting on your belt of truth and sharing your struggles (in truth with love and humility) with a fellow believer or pastor. Ask him or her to commit to praying with you and standing on Scriptures with you. You can fight this, but the Lord in his gracious wisdom doesn't usually ask us to fight our battles alone. Remember, though, that your trust should ultimately be grounded in the Lord—not in others.

In your personal battle between fear and faith, I pray that you will allow these principles to permeate your strategy. No matter who you are personally struggling with, commit to fighting your battle in the spirit. Stand on the truths of God's promises for YOUR life. Speak them even when you don't feel like it and remind your flesh of what IS true. I love this particular verse in Hebrews 10:23. *"Let us hold unswervingly to the hope we profess, for he who promised is faithful."* Your God is faithful!! Don't buy into the lies of the enemy or the "Ifs" with which he will undoubtedly taunt you. Instead, hold tightly to the truth that God is who he says he is and that he will do what he says he will do; He loves you and is ready to come to your rescue. Surrender yourself and your battle to the Lord and let him fight it for you.

I would like to prompt you to review again your personal battle and the attacks that have come at you. This is a war for your soul and over the plans that God has for your life. It is important that you do not take it lightly. The Lord has a tremendous plan for you, but it cannot come to fruition if you are drowning in fear or become exhausted fighting what feels like a losing battle. Through the Lord's grace and mercy and with the tools found in His Word, you can stand victorious in the midst of any battlefield you find yourself.

As you come to the end of this chapter, I would like you to read Psalm 146:3-9. Allow the truth of these Scriptures to sink in and take residence. The Holy Spirit may even prompt you to stand on some of these verses in your particular situation. Be encouraged that the Lord is good and full of mercy. May He grant you the strength to let go of fear and press forward towards faith.

"Do not put your trust in princes,
in human beings, who cannot save.
When their spirit departs, they return to the ground;
on that very day their plans come to nothing.
Blessed are those whose help is the God of Jacob,
whose hope is in the LORD their God.

He is the Maker of heaven and earth,
the sea, and everything in them—
he remains faithful forever.
He upholds the cause of the oppressed
and gives food to the hungry.
The LORD sets prisoners free,
the LORD gives sight to the blind,
the LORD lifts up those who are bowed down,
the LORD loves the righteous.
The LORD watches over the foreigner
and sustains the fatherless and the widow,
but he frustrates the ways of the wicked."

Your Journey. . .

1. Reflecting on your current situation(s), analyze how the enemy has attacked you, whether in your mind or through people. Has he gotten you to put your focus solely on yourself and off of God?

2. Have you started down that path of "Ifs"? Are you living in fear in your situation or in faith?

3. Oftentimes, we don't see the real fight until we begin looking for it. Are you beginning to see the real battle(s) in your own life?

4. How have you tried to fight this battle so far? Have you been fighting in the natural or in the spiritual?

5. Are you anxious or at peace?

6. Describe how you have been bound to other people's behaviors and their affects on you.

7. What would fighting this fight by faith look like?

8. How have you viewed the armor of God in the past? How are you viewing it differently now? What specifically stood out the most when we covered the armor of God?

9. In putting on your belt of truth, with whom can you share your struggles (in truth with love and humility)? Ask that friend to commit to praying with you and standing on Scriptures with you.

10. No matter who you are personally struggling with, commit to fighting your battle in the Spirit. Stand on the truths of God's promises for your life. Come before the Lord in prayer and ask Him to direct his Holy Spirit to the Scriptures you need in your tool belt.

FORGIVENESS

Chapter 11

RETURNING TO EGYPT

In Psalm 55, David writes about his betrayal by someone dear to him saying, *"If an enemy were insulting me I could endure it…but it is you…my close friend."* This chapter eerily describes the betrayer in verses 20-21, which say, *"My companion attacks his friends; he violates his covenant. His talk is smooth as butter, yet war is in his heart; his words are more soothing than oil, yet they are drawn swords."* Notice, in both references, he is speaking about the person who has wounded him deeply as his "friend" and his "companion." In verses 13-14, he says, *"But it is you, a man like myself, my companion, my close friend, with whom I once enjoyed sweet fellowship at the house of God, as we walked about among the worshipers."* This not only refers to him as a friend, but as a fellow worshiper. Someone with whom he not only shared friendship but shared one based on the foundation of the Lord. This person as described above would probably be the last person you would expect to have betrayed David.

I am thankful for this chapter, because how true is this in the church today? For many of us, it isn't the person we barely know who deeply injures us with their words or actions. It isn't the distant relative we only see on holidays, who insults our outfit, who leaves deep scars. These surface insults do inflict pain for a moment, but they typically do not leave lasting scars. However, a betrayal from a once-trusted, close friend can leave a wound so deep that if not treated can infect nearly every area of our lives. This crippling pain may very well be what led you to this book. This is the type of pain David was writing about.

As I read Psalm 55, I found myself drawn to tears, reminded of my own experiences with betrayal. Even though I have since forgiven and have truly walked out my forgiveness in this area, I can still remember the heartache. I had never experienced such raw, gut-wrenching pain as I did then. I had never felt my heart physically break until the very moment when I realized that someone I loved had utterly betrayed me. As painful as these experiences are, we can take comfort in knowing that the very same thing was experienced by David. And David, being a man after God's own heart, in his heartache, cried out to the Lord.

Verses 16-17 say, *"As for me, I call to God, and the LORD saves me. Evening, morning and noon I cry out in distress, and he hears my voice."*

In his deepest sorrow, David did not put his trust in man. No, he chose to call out to God and declared that the Lord WILL hear him! Oh, how I wish I had learned this sooner! How many times do we immediately want to pick up the phone and call a friend to share what someone has done to us? While it is true that we need encouragement from one another, people should not be our only source of comfort—nor should a person be our first point of contact. I challenge you to follow David's lead and make his declaration your own: "As for me, I call to God." The first one you should run to in your moment of distress should be the Lord.

After crying out to God in his distress, David declares the Lord's goodness and how he will uphold the righteous. In our moments of pain and heartache, or when the memory of a past betrayal comes to mind, it is imperative that we not only run to the Lord first, but that after we cry out to him, we declare his goodness and stand on his promises. David stands on many promises in this chapter, particularly about what the Lord will do to his enemies. However, one wonderful promise he stood on pertains to nearly every situation. Read verse 22:

Cast your cares on the LORD and he will sustain you; he will never let the righteous be shaken.

Praise the Lord! My friend, there will be times after you have healed from your heartbreak that the Lord will allow you to be reminded of the pain you walked through. But, his Word promises us that He will sustain us and NEVER let us be shaken! Whether during the storm or after the sky has cleared, you can plant your feet firmly on this promise and declare this truth.

After reading Psalm 55, I asked the Lord why He was reminding me of a certain situation after I finally had been able to forgive. Why was I being reminded of the pain all over again? The Lord quietly said to me, "It is so you will not forget. Forgive, yes; forget, no."

One of the enemy's greatest tools is getting us to remember our pasts the way we wish they had been instead of as they really were. In essence, drawing us to miss what we think we had in the relationship rather than focusing on the reality and moving on.

Unfortunately, I have fallen for this trick more times than I care to admit. The Lord desires not only our healing from brokenness by betrayal and loss, but also our freedom. And, freedom cannot be walked out unless we remember what we've been set free from. Even though I've forgiven the person who betrayed me, I cannot forget the betrayal. Otherwise, I risk either repeating the relationship all over again or becoming so bound by what could've been that I refuse to move forward.

I am reminded of the Israelites who, once delivered out of slavery, found themselves in a similar situation. Exodus 16:1-3 says, *"The whole Israelite community set out from Elim and came to the Desert of Sin, which is between Elim and Sinai, on the fifteenth day of the second month after they had come out of Egypt. In the desert the whole community grumbled against Moses and Aaron. The Israelites said to them, 'If only we had died by the LORD's hand in Egypt! There we sat around pots of meat and ate all the food we wanted, but you have brought us out into this desert to starve this entire assembly to death.'"* Notice, they completely left out the fact that they had been slaves in Egypt! They began to focus on the small part of the picture that had a shred of goodness to it (the food), completely forgetting the much larger picture which held the truth: they were in slavery and had been crying out to God for deliverance. Once the Lord delivered them, the enemy began to shift their focus away from what they had to what they didn't have. They petitioned Moses with various complaints, including their dislike of the available food and the lack of water. However, each time they offered a petition, the Lord was faithful to answer them. The Lord even said, *"I will rain down bread from heaven for you"* (Exodus 16:4). At one point, Moses finally said to them, *"You will know that it was the LORD when he gives you meat to eat in the evening and all the bread you want in the morning, because he has heard your grumbling against him. Who are we? You are not grumbling against us, but against the LORD"* (Exodus 16:6-8). Moses began catching on very quickly that his people were not questioning him, they were questioning God. They were doing what many of us do after we are released or "set free" from a bondage-like situation. They were looking back, remembering their captivity as they wished it had been rather than as it really was. This, in turn, caused them to look at God as a taker rather than as a giver. Accusing tones flooded their camp, and Moses was right—they were blaming their perceived problems on the One who had set them free in the first place.

You see, Egypt was home to them; it was all they'd ever known. They had been slaves, they had been mistreated and abused, but it was all they knew. It had become comfortable and familiar—it was home. As desperate as they were to escape, once freed, they longed for familiarity, no matter what it cost—even death! They began remembering a dream-version of life back in Egypt. Had they remembered the cruelty and bondage, I doubt they would've been complaining to Moses about their mundane "menu" in the desert. Instead, they would have spent their energy praising and thanking God for his mercy!

This story has held a very special place in my heart for many years. The Lord has used it numerous times to speak to me as he carried me through my own deliverance. Like the Israelites, I prayed for freedom and deliverance, prayed for the release I was given. In my own wanderings in the desert, I had prayed continually to be set free from the captivity that my heart, mind, and emotions still faced; even though I was out of that situation, I was bound mentally to it. I lived in fear and torment from nearly every new situation I faced. I was bound by an insatiable need to gain my betrayer's approval. I was bound by insecurities and unmet expectations and an endless need for affection and love. Although physically "free," I was very much still living as a captive. Perhaps you can relate.

Over the years, little by little, the Lord has patiently healed each wound that was left and has set me free from nearly every area of bondage that had restrained me. Yet, there are times when the memories come flooding back, and I find myself asking the whys and the what ifs. I replay moments in my head, rewriting the script, visualizing the way the story should have ended. I plague myself with countless scenarios and scenes in my mind of where it all went wrong and how maybe, just maybe, it could've turned out differently.

This is a very dangerous road to follow because it will lead you along the path that the ungrateful Israelites took. In doing this, you not only mourn the loss of what you did have, but you begin grieving and sometimes even obsessing over everything you didn't. Without fully being aware of it, this is what I found myself doing in regard to some of my previous relationships. Those relationships were dead and buried, yet I continued to haunt myself by digging them back up.

Let me give you a true life example of what I call "returning to Egypt." A close friend of mine (whom we will call Jane) grew up in a home filled with verbal and physical abuse. Love and safety were not traits that were found in her family, and she quickly learned that in order to survive, the only safe option was to keep to herself. Her childhood memories consist of days spent in solitude to avoid the possibility of further abuse. She cried alone, laughed alone, and felt alone the majority of her childhood. On becoming an adult, Jane found herself in a relationship similar to what she had experienced in her childhood. Abuse, violence, and mistreatment were constant, and she eventually retreated to solitude for safety. It was in this season of her life that she found the Lord and through His gentle mercy, she was delivered out of that situation. It was also during this season that we became friends. I remember her saying to me, "You're the first person who actually is showing me what love looks like." Jane would watch my husband and I in awe as she discovered what marriage and a home based on Christ can look like. With the Lord's help, she was able to get back on her own two feet and for the first time become completely self-sufficient. She became firmly grounded in the Lord and was excited at the call she was beginning to see the Lord had on her life. She began trusting again and developed wonderful friendships.

Then, somewhere along the way, something began to shift. In the stresses of supporting herself and being completely independent, Jane began looking back. All of a sudden, the rough life she had tried so desperately to leave began to look appealing. She began to question those who had poured love into her life and to pull away from the new life she had built. She no longer trusted us, her co-workers, or any of the friends she had made. In a brief moment of panic, she quit her job, left her home, and flew across the country— back to the relationships from which she had tried so desperately to gain healing and freedom. Leaving all of the ground she had covered, she put herself right back into the hands of the abuser.

I will never forget speaking to Jane on the phone after finding out what had happened. It was like talking to a completely different person. My friend was not on the other end of the phone. This person was angry and utterly gripped by fear. This person was lashing out at anyone who tried to help her or show her love.

So, what happened? I have wrestled with this question at length and lost sleep over it. Why would someone, after being delivered by God and given literally everything she had prayed and believed God for, throw it all away? There may be many reasons, but I believe one major reason is that, at some point, she began listening to the same lie that the Israelites fell for. Somewhere in the midst of her stress, she did not cry out to God as David did. She began looking at God as a taker instead of a giver. She began believing the lie that what she had back in her personal Egypt was better than the Promised Land into which the Lord was delivering her. Her history of abuse and lack of trust rose up in her and caused her to do what she would do as a child: run and hide. The problem, however, is that this time no one was abusing her. She ran from the very people who were genuinely loving and helping her. She projected her past onto her present, even though it wasn't accurate. In her mind, she believed it to be true and acted on that belief. And it cost her greatly. Both Jane and the Israelites allowed their desire for what was familiar to steal the joy of what God had given them.

The Lord desperately desires your freedom, which doesn't stop at deliverance. Whatever you have been set free from, whatever your personal Egypt may be, I cannot stress to you the importance of continually trusting the Lord through every season of it. Even when the seasons aren't pleasant or exactly as you'd like them to be, you cannot look back. It is too dangerous, and you risk running right back into slavery.

Just as the Lord did for me through Psalm 55, we have to remember the past. As for me, I can't forget the pain I was in and the daily bondage I faced. I have to keep it close to the surface because if I bury it too deeply, it could ruin me. I would naturally end up right back in slavery before I even realized what was happening. Not that I would return to the situation itself, but mentally I could become so bound to my past that it would completely affect and dictate my present life. I don't want to go back to my personal Egypt. But it is an easy place in which to find yourself if you're not careful and constantly on guard. In reading these verses in the book of Psalms, the Lord painfully reminded me where I've come from, what I've forgiven, and why I should never choose to go back.

I've also found that by not keeping the reality of my past just beneath the surface so that it is readily accessible, I can hinder my ability to minister to others. God has a beautiful way of using areas of our lives where we have been set free to help others in similar situations. The Lord has brought many people into my life who were in the midst of some very difficult situations similar to what I had walked through. God has been able to use me in their lives because I could relate to them. If I don't keep my past in its proper place, then I lose my ability to relate. If I bury the painful memories so deeply that I cannot remember them realistically, then I've lost my point of reference. How can I show someone a Savior if I can't remember what it was that He set me free from? It is not just the ability to remember, but to remember honestly. Pain, heartache, torment—it all has to remain accessible so that the Lord can use it to bring others who are hurting to Him.

Do not say, "Why were the old days better than these?" For it is not wise to ask such questions (Ecclesiastes 7:10).

Your Journey. . .

1. When have you been reminded of your past hurts?

2. Do you have a tendency to remember your past as you wish it had been, rather than as it really was? How so?

3. When confronted with memories from your past, do you cry out as David did, running to the Lord, or do you run and hide?

4. Do you remember what you've been set free from? *(Even if you've forgiven the person, list the behavior.)*

5. How have you looked at God as a taker rather than a giver?

6. Describe how you have been living as a captive to your past. How have you been bound mentally to it? (Examples: by *living in fear, needing betrayer's approval, living with insecurities, unmet expectations, relentless need for affection and love*)

7. Do you find yourself asking "why" and "what if" while replaying moments in your mind, rewriting the script the way you think the story should have played out?

8. How have you projected your past onto your present, even though it possibly isn't accurate? If you have acted on those false beliefs, what has it cost you?

9. In what ways specifically do you most identify with the Israelites?

10. Describe where you've come from, what you've forgiven, and why you would never choose to go back.

11. In what ways can you see God using your past to minister to others?

F♥RGIVENESS

Chapter 12

RESTORATION

In earlier chapters, we looked at Job and learned from his sufferings. I often get lost in Job's tragedies and forget about how Job's story ends. I believe it is only fitting that as we embark on the final chapter of this book, we look into the final chapter of Job. Job 42 is a powerful one! To refresh your memory, all of Job's family and friends had left him completely alone. He had lost everything—finances, health, social status, his children—everything. And, the only "friends" who were still talking to him were tormenting him with condemnation. In the final chapter of Job, the Lord speaks to Job's friends regarding their sin toward Job and toward the Lord. He commands them to offer a burnt sacrifice and then tells Job to pray for them (interesting, considering our study on forgiveness thus far). They did as the Lord commanded, and Job prayed for them. Starting in verse 8, we read what the Lord says to them and how he rewards Job:

The Lord says, *"I will accept [Job's] prayer and deal with you according to your folly"* (Job 42:8).

Verse 10 continues, saying, *"After Job prayed for his friends, the Lord restored his fortunes and gave him twice as much as he had before."*

And in verse 12, *"The Lord blessed the latter part of Job's life **more** than the former part"* (emphasis mine).

This is such a beautiful display of forgiveness. Job did what the Lord commanded of him; he allowed himself to be broken and humbled, continuing to walk through utter condemnation and rejection by his friends and family. And, yet, Job did as the Lord asked by being obedient, repenting before the Lord for his own sins, and then praying for his friends. In the end, the *Lord* is the one who had the final say regarding those who had wronged Job! He declared that he would *"deal with them according to their folly"* (verse 8). We know that praying for those who persecute us and have hurt us is an act of walking out forgiveness. And this is exactly what the Lord asked of Job. And what happened next?? The Lord restored Job's fortunes, giving him *twice* as much as before! Everyone who had known him came and comforted him and brought him gifts. *This* was a restored life!

Many times we are so focused on clinging to what's been lost that we fail to move forward to receive the best part! Restoration—in the Lord—**always** involves us having more than before. *"The Lord blessed the latter part more than the former"* (verse 12).

Remember, Job isn't the only lucky soul in all of history to receive this kind of restoration! The Bible is filled with promises from God for restoration. One of those promises is found in Joel 2:24-26.

The threshing floors will be filled with grain; the vats will
overflow with new wine and oil. I will repay you for the years
the locusts have eaten—the great locust and the young locust,
the other locust and the locust swarm—my great army that I
sent among you. You will have plenty to eat, until you are full,
and you will praise the name of the Lord your God who has
worked wonders for you; never again will my people be shamed.

I absolutely love this! The Lord promises to pay back the years
of harvest that the locusts destroyed. Meaning, the workers had
farmed their land, planted seeds, but were left empty-handed. The
locusts had robbed them of their harvest. Notice how God describes
each type of locust—the great, young, others, and the swarm. He
covered every type of locust (or attack) that had taken away the
crops. He said not only would he repay what had been lost but
that they would have *plenty* of food and promised fullness. In the
same way, he does this with our lives. Whatever breed of "locusts"
have robbed you of your personal "harvest," you can stand on this
promise that the Lord will be faithful to repay for the years you
have lost.

God does this to bring *praise* and *glory* to his name, according to
verse 26. He works *wonders* on our behalf so that we may praise him!
If our hearts are not operating in full capacity, surrendered to him
through our brokenness, repentance, and forgiveness, we cannot
receive his full restoration. Why? Because of his two-fold purpose:
first of all, he restores us because of his unrelenting love for us as his
children. He longs to be near to us, to know us, and to be known
by us. Second, he restores us to bring *himself* glory and shine a light

so brightly through us that we reflect what only he can do—the miraculous. We become walking, breathing, living testimonials of what the power of God can do. However, if we are still withholding portions of ourselves and clinging to our pain, we cannot bring full glory to God. We must come to full surrender, like Job, in order to be fully restored and bring God the fullness of our praise.

Another promise is found in 1 Peter 5:10.

And the God of grace who called you to his eternal glory in Christ, after you have suffered a little while, will himself restore you and make you strong, firm and steadfast.

I love this verse because it reminds me that no acts of righteousness can deem us "worthy" of being restored. It is only by the grace of God and through the mercy of Jesus Christ that we are ever restored.

I want you to go back with me into time, and imagine if you will, a woman at the foot of the cross. This woman isn't anyone special or prominent. She lives a seemingly normal life for her day, working and doing what she can to get by. Yet, like many of us, she carries the weight of a battered and wounded soul. She may have been the victim of abuse or mistreatment; she may have been abandoned by people she loved. She may have suffered great loss and heartache; she may have been wronged unjustly— no one really knows her story except God.

At this moment, she finds herself on her knees with her face in the dirt, soaking the ground with her tears, clawing at the gravel and rocks in the ground in utter and complete torment due to the anguish in her soul. Realizing the full weight of the price being paid by Jesus for her, she can't even bear to look up. She weeps into the dirt, begging and pleading for him to extend his grace toward her. She inches closer, knowing that if one drop of his blood could fall upon her, she would be restored; she would be healed and made whole.

Without looking up, she presses her face into the ground, feeling completely unworthy of what she is about to ask. Smelling the tear-stained earth beneath her, with every ounce of strength left in her lungs, she cries out for mercy. She weeps at the foot of the cross that bears her dying Savior. Ever so gently, a drop of blood falls from his wounded body onto her wounded life. And, she is restored.

Although this story is fictitious, it feels very real. We do not have the opportunity to physically go to the foot of the cross, but spiritually we do. When we cry out for mercy, we become like this woman and spiritually find ourselves just like her, with our faces in the dirt before the cross. Then, in his infinite mercy, Jesus allows his blood to cover us. The blood from his broken body is our key to walking in forgiveness and freedom. Without the power of his blood, our attempts to restore our life will fall short.

In 1 Peter 5, we are *"called to his eternal glory in Christ."* What brings glory to the Lord? A restored life. A life that has been supernaturally restored by the miraculous grace of God—with no other explanation possible. That brings him eternal glory! The verse goes onto say that Christ *"himself will restore you and make you strong, firm and steadfast."* Christ himself did this on the cross. He took all the pain; he was beaten, he bled, and he died in order to restore your broken life. He did it by his grace. When we cry for his mercy out of our broken, humbled state, his blood extends from that cross onto our lives. What a beautiful Savior!

There is one question that I have purposefully not addressed until now. You may know which one it is, because you may have secretly wondered the same thing yourself. "Why did God let these things happen to me?" In order for me to fully give my answer, I felt that you needed to read the previous chapters first, and also the first part of this chapter, to understand the context in which my answer is given.

I am so thankful for God's Word, particularly pertaining to this subject. His Word is tried, tested, and true. It is so easy to be pulled astray and fall into the traps and lies of this world, landing yourself in the pit of confusion. Without the Word of God as a guide and clear map with which to maneuver, I would be utterly lost as to how to answer this question. As always, we must turn to God's Word.

*In all this you greatly rejoice, though now for a little while you may have had to suffer grief in all kinds of trials. **These have come** so that the proven genuineness of your faith—of greater worth than gold, which perishes even though refined by fire—may result in praise, glory and honor when Jesus Christ is revealed. Though you have not seen him, you love him; and even though you do not see him now, you believe in him and are filled with an inexpressible and glorious joy, for you are receiving the end result of your faith, the salvation of your souls* (1 Peter 1:6–9).

There are many verses that I hold dear to my heart, but this one just might be my favorite. This describes my journey better than any words I could formulate ever could. People have asked me why I think God allowed me to go through what I did and whether I thought it was God's punishment for something wrong I had done. And for a while, I honestly wasn't sure. Sometimes we do reap painful consequences from our choices—choices that we have made which are in direct disobedience to the guidelines laid out for us in God's Word. Yet other times, for no obvious reason, bad things happen to good people. For no reason at all, loving, giving, Christ-following believers may find themselves the object of abuse, torment, and mistreatment. And we find ourselves saying, "Okay, God…why?" Having studied the Word and particularly this verse, I believe in many cases we aren't being punished, nor have we simply been forgotten by God. If we believe the Word of God to be the truth, then we must take this verse as such and apply it as a litmus test to our question. 1 Peter tells us that *"these [trials] have come so that your faith may be proven genuine."* It says our faith is worth far more than gold and that the goal of our faith is to be filled with an inexpressible joy through the salvation of our souls.

I am just now beginning to grasp the weight of this. During some difficult seasons of my life that seemed to leave me with more questions than answers, this verse radiated truth and offered a "light bulb moment" for me that I otherwise would not have had. You see, long before I was ever aware, the Lord had a plan, a purpose, and a calling over my life. I now know that it was to reach those who are deeply wounded and hurting. I was called to write, speak, and to counsel others, utilizing what the Lord has done in my life.

That was the plan all along. But, how could I reach that goal without having experienced what I was called to minister? How could I have written a book about forgiveness if I'd never had to walk through it? How could I speak about freedom and deliverance if I'd never been in captivity? How could I minister in healing if I'd never been wounded?

We tend to take a quick "snapshot" of our life in one moment of pain or heartache and throw up our hands and say, "Well, I must have missed God" or "That's it. God has completely forgotten about me." Instead of looking at the entire picture and striving to see it from God's perspective, we focus on that "moment" and wring our hands, wondering where it all went wrong.

Now that I'm on the other side of suffering "grief in all kinds of trials," I have a refined faith that is worth far more than gold to me and an "inexpressible and glorious joy" that others do not understand. I cannot explain it outside the healing work of Jesus. Why do I have this joy? Because I am "receiving the goal of my faith." I am receiving restoration. I am living a life where my "latter half is greater than the first."   This is not just for me—this promise is for you. This is who God is, and this is what he does; he restores our broken pieces into something far greater than before. And, sometimes, the pain actually has a purpose—one that far outweighs anything you could possibly imagine. Personally, I would take all of the pain, heartache, and grief all over again to have the relationship with the Lord that I am walking in today. I am finally walking in my calling, and it is amazing. But, I would not be here today had I not first walked through every unjust, unfair, treacherous heartache that I experienced. What I am asking you to consider is the possibility of a purpose behind the pain. Psalm 119:71 puts it this way:

It was good for me to be afflicted so
that I might learn your decrees.

When we suffer through trials and grief, if we choose to surrender our pain to the Lord and walk in obedience to His Word through everything as we've discussed, we will come to this place of complete dependency on Him that we otherwise would not have known. That is what this verse is describing. When we arrive at that place, restoration has begun taking place. These words readily flow out of a restored person's mouth. Why? Because they have captured that faith which has become more precious to them than any gold or earthly treasure. They are walking in that "inexpressible joy" and wouldn't trade it for anything else in this world. The 71st Psalm gives another example of this kind of dependence on the Lord.

Though you have made me see troubles, many and
bitter, you will restore my life again; from the depths of
the earth you will again bring me up (Psalm 71:20).

When I read this, I hear it with such determination! By writing this, the author assumed God had a purpose behind the pain, because he was demanding that God hold true to His promise and restore him *again*. This tells me that the author had encountered these trials before. The author knew God, knew his character, and knew his consistency in this matter. He knew that he was being refined; instead of questioning God on it, he embraced it! He told God what God would do because he KNEW God's faithfulness in this area could be trusted.

Chapter 9 in the book of Amos provides another glimpse of the consistency of this promise. In verses 8-10, God says he will *"shake the people of Israel … as grain is shaken in a sieve."* This adequately describes the breaking process the Lord allows us to go through in order to refine us. In verse 11, he goes on to describe restoration.

> *In that day, I will restore David's fallen*
> *shelter—I will repair its broken walls*
> *and restore its ruins—and will rebuild*
> *it as it used to be* (Amos 9:11).

Continuing in verses 14-15, he gives his promise to the people:
They will rebuild the ruined cities and live in them. They will plant vineyards and drink their wine; they will make gardens and eat their fruit. I will plant Israel in their own land, never again to be uprooted from the land I have given them.

Notice how God emphasizes that He is the one doing the planting. When we plant ourselves—or rather, when we try to "fix" or "repair" ourselves—we will undoubtedly come to ruin again. Once you've been planted by the Lord, it is nearly impossible to be uprooted. This doesn't mean that you will never face trials again—possibly even some similar ones. The difference will be that they will not uproot you again. The Lord does not force anyone to do what's right—which includes those with whom you are in a relationship now and those with whom you could have a potential relationship in the future. What the Lord *can* promise is that once you've been broken and have allowed him to rebuild you and replant you, you will *live* and *thrive* there—no matter what chaos transpires around you. You will enjoy the fruit of your labor and the work of your hands, and you will never be uprooted from your land again! You will not only stand firm but also sing of the Lord's praises for what he has done in your life. Like the psalmist in Psalm 26:12 declares:

My feet stand on level ground; in the great
assembly I will praise the Lord.

My friend, this is my prayer for you and the heartbeat behind each and every page of this book. I know these promises to be true and pray that the Lord will heal you and plant your feet firmly in Him so that you will never again be shaken. I pray that, as it was with Job, your latter days will be better than your former. My prayer for you is that these will be your words:

I run in the path of your commands for you
have set my heart free (Psalm 119: 32).

Once you have been healed and your heart has truly been set free, you will not only cling to God's Word but will RUN with it. There is such a tremendous safety that comes in the rest that can only be found in that intimate place of healing with the Lord.

I want to share with you a portion of lyrics to a song whose cry has beautifully resounded in my heart throughout this journey. Music has such a unique way of capturing the very essence of what we are experiencing; this song has done that for me. Many days I have sung this at the top of my lungs as my newly freed heart began to stretch its wings. This perfectly describes where I have been, where I am today, and what I pray will be the same for you. The following chorus is excerpted from "What I've Overcome" by Fireflight:

"If only you could see me yesterday
Who I used to be before the change
You'd see a broken heart
You'd see the battle scars

Funny how words can't explain
How good it feels to break the chains
I'm not what I have done
I'm what I've overcome"

As we close this book, I would like to do something a little un-conventional. We have journeyed together, and I have shared with you some intimate details of my life which I hope have encouraged your heart to surrender to Jesus, allowing him to heal you and begin restoring your life. At this time, I want to encourage you to take a moment and let the magnitude of the Cross sink in. We are able to ask for healing and restoration only because of what Jesus did on that cross. I invite you to sit and take communion with the Lord. It doesn't have to be fancy or religious; it will be between you and God alone. No pretenses, no games. When you break the bread and drink the wine/juice symbolizing his broken body and blood spilled to offer healing to your life, imagine yourself like that woman at the foot of the cross at the beginning of this chapter. Imagine yourself with your face in the dirt, utterly in need of the Savior. Cry out to him, thanking him for what he endured for your freedom.

> *I remain confident of this:*
>   *I will see the goodness of the LORD*
> (Psalm 27:13).

Your Journey. . .

1. What new perspectives have you gained from looking over the life of Job and how his story ended? Journal your thoughts here.

2. Re-read Joel 2:24-26. What have been the locusts in your life? According to this passage, what does God promise he will do in these areas of your life?

3. Review 1 Peter 1:6-9. What did you take from this passage, and how did it challenge you?

4. What purpose(s) do you think there could be behind your pain?

5. In what ways could you see yourself reaching out to others who are suffering in the same areas as you have suffered?

6. Re-read Amos 9:14-15. In what ways have you tried to "plant" (restore) yourself? What does God's Word promise us when we allow God to plant us?

7. Pray and ask the Lord to reveal to you his plan for your pain. Memorize Psalm 71:20.

F♥RGIVENESS

SCRIPTURE REFERENCES BY CHAPTER

Chapter One:

The Israelites grieved for Moses in the plains of Moab thirty days, until the time of weeping and mourning was over.

(Deuteronomy 34:8)

I tell you the truth, you will weep and mourn while the world rejoices. You will grieve, but your grief will turn to joy. A woman giving birth to a child has pain because her time has come; but when her baby is born she forgets the anguish because of her joy that a child is born into the world. So with you: Now is your time of grief, but I will see you again and you will rejoice, and no one will take away your joy.

(John 16:20-22)

Chapter Two:

*No, in all these things we are more than conquerors through
him who loved us. For I am convinced that neither death
nor life, neither angels nor demons, neither the present nor
the future, nor any powers, neither height nor depth, nor
anything else in all creation, will be able to separate us
from the love of God that is in Christ Jesus our Lord.*

(Romans 8:37–39)

*I have loved you with an everlasting love; I
have drawn you with unfailing kindness.*

(Jeremiah 31:3)

*The Spirit of the Sovereign LORD is on me, because the
LORD has anointed me to proclaim good news to the poor.
He has sent me to bind up the brokenhearted, to proclaim
freedom for the captives and release from darkness for the
prisoners, to proclaim the year of the LORD's favor and the
day of vengeance of our God, to comfort all who mourn, and
provide for those who grieve in Zion—to bestow on them
a crown of beauty instead of ashes, the oil of joy instead of
mourning, and a garment of praise instead of a spirit of despair.*

(Isaiah 61:1–3)

*Oh, that my words were recorded, that they were written
on a scroll, that they were inscribed with an iron tool on
lead, or engraved in rock forever! I know that my redeemer
lives, and that in the end he will stand on the earth. And
after my skin has been destroyed, yet in my flesh I will*

see God; I myself will see him with my own eyes—I,
and not another. How my heart yearns within me.

(Job 19: 23-27)

The waters closed over my head, and I thought I was about to
perish. I called on your name, LORD, from the depths of the
pit. You heard my plea: "Do not close your ears to my cry for
relief." You came near when I called you, and you said, "Do
not fear." You, Lord, took up my case; you redeemed my life.

(Lamentations 3:54-58)

Chapter 3

May they be put to shame for wronging me without cause...

(Psalm 119:78)

Why, LORD, do you stand far off? Why do you hide yourself
in times of trouble? In his arrogance the wicked man hunts
down the weak, who are caught in the schemes he devises. He
boasts about the cravings of his heart; he blesses the greedy and
reviles the LORD. In his pride the wicked man does not seek
him; in all his thoughts there is no room for God. His ways are
always prosperous; your laws are rejected by him; he sneers at all
his enemies. He says to himself, "Nothing will ever shake me."
He swears, "No one will ever do me harm." His mouth is full
of lies and threats; trouble and evil are under his tongue. He lies
in wait near the villages; from ambush he murders the innocent.
His eyes watch in secret for his victims; like a lion in cover he
lies in wait. He lies in wait to catch the helpless; he catches the
helpless and drags them off in his net. His victims are crushed,

they collapse; they fall under his strength. He says to himself,
"God will never notice; he covers his face and never sees."

(Psalm 10:1-11)

But you, God, see the trouble of the afflicted; you consider
their grief and take it in hand. The victims commit
themselves to you; you are the helper of the fatherless. Break
the arm of the wicked man; call the evildoer to account for
his wickedness that would not otherwise be found out.

(Psalm 10:14-15)

The LORD is King for ever and ever; the nations will
perish from his land. You, LORD, hear the desire of
the afflicted; you encourage them, and you listen to their
cry, defending the fatherless and the oppressed, so that
mere earthly mortals will never again strike terror.

(Psalm 10:16-18)

But I will restore you to health and heal your
wounds, declares the Lord, because you are called
an outcast, Zion for whom no one cares.

(Jeremiah 30:17)

Chapter 4

Because of all my enemies, I am the utter contempt of my
neighbors and an object of dread to my closest friends— those
who see me on the street flee from me. I am forgotten as
though I were dead; I have become like broken pottery.

(Psalm 31:11-13)

My sacrifice, O God, is a broken spirit; a broken
and contrite heart you, God, will not despise.

(Psalm 51:17)

The LORD is close to the brokenhearted and
saves those who are crushed in spirit.

(Psalm 34:18)

Chapter 5

The sins of some are obvious, reaching the place of judgment
ahead of them; the sins of others trail behind them. In
the same way, good deeds are obvious, and even those
that are not obvious cannot remain hidden forever.

(1 Timothy 5:24-25)

A good name is more desirable than riches; to
be esteemed is better than silver or gold.

(Proverbs 22:1)

Do not be misled. Bad company corrupts good character.

(1 Corinthians 15:33)

This is the covenant I will establish with the people of Israel
after that time, declares the Lord. I will put my laws in their
minds and write them on their hearts. I will be their God, and
they will be my people No longer will they teach their neighbor,
or say to one another, "Know the Lord," because they will
all know me, from the least of them to the greatest. For I will
forgive their wickedness and will remember their sins no more.

(Hebrews 8:10-12)

So from now on we regard no one from a worldly point of
view. Though we once regarded Christ in this way, we do
so no longer. Therefore, if anyone is in Christ, the new
creation has come: The old has gone, the new is here!

(2 Corinthians 5:16-17)

Chapter 6

For if you forgive other people when they sin against you,
your heavenly Father will also forgive you. But if you do not
forgive others their sins, your Father will not forgive your sins.

(Matthew 6:14-15)

Jesus said, "Father, forgive them, for they
do not know what they are doing."

(Luke 23:34)

In him we have redemption through his blood, the
forgiveness of sins, in accordance with the riches
of God's grace that he lavished on us.

(Ephesians 1:7-8)

For God so loved the world that he gave his one and only Son, that whoever believes in him shall not perish but have eternal life. For God did not send his Son into the world to condemn the world, but to save the world through him.

(John 3:16–17)

Suggested reading: Luke 23

Chapter 7

And now these three remain: faith, hope and love. But the greatest of these is love.

(1 Corinthians 13:13)

But I tell you, love your enemies and pray for those who persecute you.

(Matthew 5:44)

But to you who are listening I say: Love your enemies, do good to those who hate you.

(Luke 6:27)

But love your enemies, do good to them, and lend to them without expecting to get anything back. Then your reward will be great, and you will be children of the Most High, because he is kind to the ungrateful and wicked.

(Luke 6:35)

In doing this, you will heap burning coals on his head, and the LORD will reward you."

(Proverbs 25:22)

Instead, speaking the truth in love, we will grow
to become in every respect the mature body of
him who is the head, that is, Christ.

(Ephesians 4:15)

Therefore each of you must put off falsehood
and speak truthfully to your neighbor.

(Ephesians 4:25)

Love is patient, love is kind. It does not envy, it does not
boast, it is not proud. It is not rude, it is not self-seeking, it is
not easily angered, it keeps no record of wrongs. Love does not
delight in evil, but rejoices with the truth. It always protects,
always trusts, always hopes, always perseveres. Love never fails.

(1 Corinthians 13:4-8)

A fool shows his annoyance at once, but a
prudent man over looks an insult.

(Proverbs 12:16)

A prudent man keeps his knowledge to himself,
but the heart of fools blurts out folly.

(Proverbs 12:23)

But love your enemies, do good to them, and lend to
them without expecting to get anything back. Then your
reward will be great, and you will be children of the Most
High, because he is kind to the ungrateful and wicked.

(Luke 6:35)

*We were under great pressure far beyond our ability to
endure, so that we despaired even of life. Indeed in our
hearts we felt the sentence of death. But this happened that
we might not rely on ourselves but on God, who raises
the dead. He has delivered us from such peril, and he will
deliver us. On Him, we have set our hope that He will
continue to deliver us, as you help us by your prayers.*

(2 Corinthians 1:8-10)

Chapter 8

*[Jesus] asked him, "Do you want to get well?" "Sir," the
invalid replied, "I have no one to help me into the pool
when the water is stirred. While I am trying to get in,
someone else goes down ahead of me." Then Jesus said
it him, "Get up! Pick up your mat and walk." At once
the man was cured; he picked up his mat and walked.*

(John 5:6-8)

*I sought the Lord and He answered me; he delivered
me from all my fears. Those who look to Him are
radiant; their faces are never covered with shame.*

(Psalm 34:4-5)

No one will be condemned who takes refuge in Him.

(Psalm 34:22)

*A righteous man may have many troubles, but
the Lord delivers him from them all.*

(Psalm 34:19)

The righteous cry out and the Lord hears them…He is
close to the brokenhearted and saves the crushed in spirit.

(Psalm 34:17-18)

The end of a matter is better than the beginning.

(Ecclesiastes 7:8)

Chapter 9

Who shall separate us from the love of Christ?
Shall trouble or hardship or persecution or
famine or nakedness or danger or sword?

(Romans 8:35)

Now in all these things we are more than conquerors
through Him who loved us. For I am convinced that
neither death nor life, neither angels nor demons, neither
the present nor the future not any powers, neither
height nor depth, nor anything else in all creation
will be able to separate us from the love of God.

(Romans 8:37-39)

Then Jesus was led by the Spirit into the wilderness to be
tempted by the devil. After fasting forty days and forty
nights, he was hungry. The tempter came to him and
said, "If you are the Son of God, tell these stones to become
bread." Jesus answered, "It is written: 'Man shall not live
on bread alone, but on every word that comes from the mouth
of God.'" Then the devil took him to the holy city and had
him stand on the highest point of the temple. "If you are

*the Son of God," he said, "throw yourself down. For it is
written: 'He will command his angels concerning you, and
they will lift you up in their hands, so that you will not
strike your foot against a stone.'" Jesus answered him, "It is
also written: 'Do not put the Lord your God to the test'."*

(Matthew 4:1-7)

*Again, the devil took him to a very high mountain and showed
him all the kingdoms of the world and their splendor. "All this
I will give you," he said, "if you will bow down and worship
me." Jesus said to him, "Away from me, Satan! For it is
written: 'Worship the Lord your God, and serve him only.'"
Then the devil left him, and angels came and attended him.*

(Matthew 4:8-11)

*I have hidden your word in my heart
that I might not sin against you.*

(Psalm 119:11)

For the mouth speaks what the heart is full of.

(Matthew 12:34)

*It is impossible for God to lie, we who have fled to take hold
of the hope set before us may be greatly encouraged. We
have this hope as an anchor for the soul, firm and secure.*

(Hebrews 6:18-19)

Chapter 10

*For our struggle is not against flesh and blood, but
against the rulers, against the authorities, against
the powers of this dark world and against the
spiritual forces of evil in the heavenly realms.*

(Ephesians 6:12)

*For though we live in the world, we do not wage war as the
world does. The weapons we fight with are not the weapons
of the world. On the contrary, they have divine power to
demolish strongholds. We demolish arguments and every
pretension that sets itself up against the knowledge of God, and
we take captive every thought to make it obedient to Christ.*

(1 Corinthians 10:3-5)

*Therefore put on the full armor of God, so that when the day
of evil comes, you may be able to stand your ground, and after
you have done everything, to stand. Stand firm then, with the
belt of truth buckled around your waist, with the breastplate
of righteousness in place, and with your feet fitted with the
readiness that comes from the gospel of peace. In addition to all
this, take up the shield of faith, with which you can extinguish
all the flaming arrows of the evil one. Take the helmet of
salvation and the sword of the Spirit, which is the word of God.*

(Ephesians 6:13-17)

*Ask and it will be given to you; seek and you will
find; knock and the door will be opened to you.*

(Matthew 7:7)

Though one may be overpowered, two can defend themselves. A cord of three strands is not quickly broken.

(Ecclesiastes 4:12)

Let us hold unswervingly to the hope we profess, for he who promised is faithful.

(Hebrews 10:23)

Do not put your trust in princes, in human beings, who cannot save. When their spirit departs, they return to the ground; on that very day their plans come to nothing. Blessed are those whose help is the God of Jacob, whose hope is in the LORD their God. He is the Maker of heaven and earth, the sea, and everything in them—he remains faithful forever. He upholds the cause of the oppressed and gives food to the hungry. The LORD sets prisoners free, the LORD gives sight to the blind, the LORD lifts up those who are bowed down, the LORD loves the righteous. The LORD watches over the foreigner and sustains the fatherless and the widow, but he frustrates the ways of the wicked.

(Psalm 146:3-9)

Chapter 11

If an enemy were insulting me, I could endure it; if a foe were rising against me, I could hide. But it is you, a man like myself, my companion, my close friend.

(Psalm 55:12-13)

*But it is you, a man like myself, my companion, my close
friend, with whom I once enjoyed sweet fellowship at the
house of God, as we walked about among the worshipers.*

(Psalm 55:13-14)

*As for me, I call to God, and the LORD saves me. Evening,
morning and noon I cry out in distress, and he hears my voice.*

(Psalm 55:16-17)

*Cast your cares on the LORD and he will sustain
you; he will never let the righteous be shaken.*

(Psalm 55:22)

*The whole Israelite community set out from Elim and came to
the Desert of Sin, which is between Elim and Sinai, on the
fifteenth day of the second month after they had come out of
Egypt. In the desert the whole community grumbled against
Moses and Aaron. The Israelites said to them, "If only we had
died by the LORD's hand in Egypt! There we sat around pots
of meat and ate all the food we wanted, but you have brought
us out into this desert to starve this entire assembly to death."*

(Exodus 16:1-3)

*"You will know that it was the LORD when he gives you meat
to eat in the evening and all the bread you want in the morning,
because he has heard your grumbling against him. Who are we?
You are not grumbling against us, but against the LORD."*

(Exodus 16:6-8)

Do not say, "Why were the old days better than
these?" For it is not wise to ask such questions.

(Ecclesiastes 7:10)

Chapter 12

"I will accept his [Job's] prayer and deal
with you according to your folly."

(Job 42:8)

After Job prayed for his friends, the Lord restored his
fortunes and gave him twice as much as he had before.

(Job 42:10)

The Lord blessed the latter part of Job's
life more than the former part.

(Job 42:12)

The threshing floors will be filled with grain; the vats will
overflow with new wine and oil. I will repay you for the years
the locusts have eaten – the great locust and the young locust,
the other locust and the locust swarm – my great army that I
sent among you. You will have plenty to eat, until you are full,
and you will praise the name of the Lord your God who has
worked wonders for you; never again will my people be shamed.

(Joel 2:24-26)

And the God of grace who called you to his eternal glory in
Christ, after you have suffered a little while, will himself
restore you and make you strong, firm and steadfast.

(1 Peter 5:10)

*In all this you greatly rejoice, though now for a little while
you may have had to suffer grief in all kinds of trials. These
have come so that the proven genuineness of your faith—of
greater worth than gold, which perishes even though refined by
fire—may result in praise, glory and honor when Jesus Christ
is revealed. Though you have not seen him, you love him; and
even though you do not see him now, you believe in him and
are filled with an inexpressible and glorious joy, for you are
receiving the end result of your faith, the salvation of your souls.*

(1 Peter 1:6-9)

*It was good for me to be afflicted so that I might learn
your decrees. The law from your mouth is more precious
to me than thousands of pieces of silver and gold.*

(Psalm 119:71-72)

*Though you have made me see troubles, many
and bitter, you will restore my life again; from the
depths of the earth you will again bring me up.*

(Psalm 71:20)

*In that day, I will restore David's fallen shelter—I
will repair its broken walls and restore its ruins
—and will rebuild it as it used to be.*

(Amos 9:11)

They will rebuild the ruined cities and live in them. They will plant vineyards and drink their wine; they will make gardens and eat their fruit. I will plant Israel in their own land, never again to be uprooted from the land I have given them.

(Amos 9:14-15)

My feet stand on level ground; in the great assembly I will praise the Lord.

(Psalm 26:12)

I run in the path of your commands for you have set my heart free.

(Psalm 119:32)

I remain confident of this: I will see the goodness of the LORD.

(Psalm 27:13)

F♥RGIVENESS

SPECIAL THANKS

I would like to thank Brenda, Jonathan, Mom, Memee, and Teresa for being my right-hand editing team! Your insight and suggestions helped shape this creative project into what it is. Your careful attention to detail was such a gift, and the time you dedicated to helping this work come to life was truly astounding. Thank you! Thank you to Fireflight for writing music that in many ways was the anthem to this project and this season of my life. To my wonderful parents and in-laws, thank you for the countless hours in helping with my girls so I could take the time to write. Without you, this simply would not have been possible! To my husband Zac, thank you for believing in this project and for believing in me. Your love and devotion are the heartbeat of our family in so many ways. I love and appreciate you so much. And, most importantly, thank you, Jesus, for restoring my broken life and for shining your light through me. You are the reason for my joy and the source of my strength. Without you, I am but an empty, broken piece of pottery. It is because of you that I have been restored. Thank you!

To download a free Leader Study Guide
or to learn more about
ANNA MCCARTHY
&
VOICE OF ONE MINISTRIES
please visit:

www.voiceofone.net
@Vof1Ministry
www.facebook.com/voiceofoneministry

....

For more information about
AMBASSADOR INTERNATIONAL
please visit:

www.ambassador-international.com
@AmbassadorIntl
www.facebook.com/AmbassadorIntl